DATE DUE

EVOLUTION
THE BASICS

Evolution: The Basics is an engaging introduction to the history, development and science of the theory of evolution. Beginning pre-Darwin and concluding with the latest research and controversies, readers are introduced to the origins of the idea of evolution, the ways in which it has developed and been adapted over time, and the science underpinning it all. Topics addressed include:

- Early theories of evolution
- The impact of Darwin's *On the Origin of Species*
- The discovery of genetics and Mendel's experiments
- Molecular evolution and the discovery of DNA
- The expansion of life and the persistence of disease
- Revisiting evolutionary ethics and the development of empathy.

Evolution: The Basics examines the role of evolution in current debates and discusses the possible future developments in the field. This book is invaluable reading for all students and individuals seeking to understand the wide-ranging sphere of evolutionary theory.

Sherrie Lyons is Assistant Professor at the Center for Distance Learning of Empire State College, State University of New York. She is author of *Species, Serpents, Spirits, and Skulls: Science at the Margins in the Victorian Age* and *Thomas Henry Huxley: The Evolution of a Scientist*.

The Basics

EVOLUTION

THE BASICS

sherrie lyons

LONDON AND NEW YORK

First published 2011
by Routledge
2 Park Square, Milton Park, Abingdon, Oxon OX14 4RN

Simultaneously published in the USA and Canada
by Routledge
711 Third Avenue, New York, NY 10017

Routledge is an imprint of the Taylor & Francis Group, an informa business

British Library Cataloguing in Publication Data
A catalogue record for this book is available from the British Library

Library of Congress Cataloging in Publication Data
Lyons, Sherrie Lynne, 1947-
  Evolution / Sherrie Lyons.
    p. cm. – (The basics)
  Includes bibliographical references.
  1. Evolution (Biology) I. Title.
  QH367.L956 2012
  576.8–dc22
                    2011002891

ISBN: 978-0-415-59225-3 (hbk)
ISBN: 978-0-415-59226-0 (pbk)
ISBN: 978-0-203-80806-1 (ebk)

Typeset in Bembo and Scalasans
by Taylor & Francis Books

CONTENTS

FIGURES

ACKNOWLEDGEMENTS

FIGURES 2.1, 2.2

Reproduced with permission from John van Wyhe ed., The Complete Work of Charles Darwin Online (http://darwin-online. org.uk/)

FIGURE 3.1

© 2004 *Human Evolutionary Genetics*, by M. A. Jobling, M. E. Hurles and C. Tyler-Smith.
Reproduced by permission of Garland Science/Taylor & Francis LLC.

FIGURES 3.2

© 2002 *Genetics for Healthcare Professionals*, by Heather Skirton and Christine Patch.
Reproduced by permission of Garland Science/Taylor & Francis LLC.

FIGURES 4.1, 4.2

© 2008 *Molecular Biology of the Cell*, 5th edn, by Bruce Alberts et al.
Reproduced by permission of Garland Science/Taylor & Francis LLC.

INTRODUCTION

WHY STUDY EVOLUTION?

Evolution is the great unifying **theory** for biology. No idea in biology has been more scientifically powerful. Evolution has in the past and continues today to provide a research program in diverse fields including **paleontology**, molecular biology, **embryology**, ecology, human behavior, and medicine. It has impacted other fields as well, from computer animation software design to economic theory. Because of this, evolution is increasingly relevant for understanding human society. Evolution is not just about dinosaurs and **fossils** or our common ancestry with apes. Evolutionary ideas have provided insight into topics such as decision-making, mating habits, morality, mental illness, and religion. It explains why most of us love the taste of foods that are high in fat, salt, and sugar. It helps elucidate why we are capable of both extremely selfish and unselfish behavior, exhibit both honesty and deceit, and are sometimes spiteful while at other times forgiving. Evolution reveals that we are all interconnected in the great web of life and can provide guidance in taking care of our amazing planet earth. Charles Darwin's good friend Thomas Huxley (1825–95) wrote over 100 years ago, there is "no field of biological inquiry in which the influence of the 'Origin of Species' is not traceable" and that "as the embodiment of an **hypothesis** it is destined to be the guide of biological and psychological speculation for the next three or four generations." Huxley's words were prophetic.

THE MEANING OF EVOLUTION

Life on earth today is the result of its ever-changing complex history that began billions of years ago. However, this idea is a relatively recent development in Western thought. The Christian world view from the Middle Ages almost up to Darwin's time held that the world was both constant and of short duration. The idea of evolution, i.e. that **species** change over time, had been around since the early Greeks, but it was not until 1859 with Darwin's publication of *On the Origin of Species by Means of Natural Selection, or the Preservation of Favoured Races in the Struggle for Life* that evolution became widely accepted. The word evolution has an interesting history, coming from the Latin infinitive *evolvere* meaning "to unfold or disclose." Evolution in the late 1600s was used to describe embryological development. In 1744 Albrecht von Haller (1708–77) applied the term evolution to characterize the preformationist embryology of the Dutch entomologist Jan Swammerdam (1637–80). **Preformation** held that all the organs and internal parts existed fully formed in the embryo and just had to be augmented and expanded. This contrasted with **epigenesis** in which the organs of higher animals developed sequentially, gradually changing from an undifferentiated state to a highly differentiated state. By the 1800s evolution became associated with this latter view, a kind of progressive embryological development. Naturalists also started to apply the ideas from embryology to the fossil record and claimed that the development of species recapitulated the development of the individual, i.e. the development of more complex organisms over time repeated the stages of embryonic development observed in an individual animal. Evolution came to mean both embryological and species progression, and it did not mean that one species actually transformed into another. Rather than "evolution," the term **transmutation** was used for species transformation. In fact, many naturalists such as William Carpenter (1813–85) and Richard Owen (1804–92) who supported a developmental view of the fossil record argued specifically against the idea of transmutation. However, the ideas of development and transmutation are clearly not incompatible. Darwin recognized the importance of development and thought that embryology provided the strongest evidence in favor of his theory. After Darwin the word evolution became exclusively associated with the idea of descent with modification. How does such a process occur? Darwin argued, first, that organisms vary and some of the variations are inherited. Second, there is a struggle for existence. Third, those organisms that have more favorable variations in the struggle will survive in greater numbers and most importantly leave more offspring. Thus (fourth), over time those favorable traits will be selected for and will spread though the population, eventually resulting in new species emerging. Thus for evolution to occur there must be (1) variation, (2) inheritance, and (3) selection. Ernst Mayr (1904–2005) has written that Darwin's theory contains five sub-theories that relate to different aspects of variational evolution. These are: (1) organisms evolve or change over time, (2) different organisms have descended from a common ancestor, (3) species multiply over time or speciation, (4) evolution is slow and gradual, (5) the primary mechanism of evolutionary change is **natural selection**. While descent from a common ancestor was relatively quickly accepted in Darwin's time, his mechanism of natural selection was not. It was not until the 1940s, a period that became known as the Modern Synthesis, that natural selection was vindicated as the primary mechanism of evolution. However, the role of development was essentially ignored in the synthesis period. It is only relatively recently that research from embryology has been used to extend our understanding of evolutionary processes. In doing so evolutionary developmental biology or **evo-devo** is uniting the many different meanings evolution has had through its own evolutionary history and providing an ever deepening understanding of the history of life.

EVOLUTION AS A SCIENTIFIC THEORY

Critics of evolution often will say that it is "only a theory." What does this mean? When scientists use the word theory, it has a much different meaning than in common parlance. Scientific theories provide a means of understanding the natural world. Without an overarching theory, we may make countless observations, but we will not understand what we are seeing. Scientists do not just adopt any theory because they like it. The first important aspect of scientific theories is they provide a framework for solving particular problems. Evolution became the great unifying theory in biology precisely because it solved so many problems that confronted working biologists. Developing theories is fundamentally what scientists do in much the same way that politicians develop policies. We do not say to a politician that his/her policy on welfare is "only" a policy. More relevant, we do not claim that gravity is "only" a theory of gravity. Yet there is as much evidence for the theory of evolution as there is for gravity, so why do people say it is "only" a theory? Nevertheless, just as welfare policies can change, scientific theories also change as new evidence comes in. Newton's laws apply well to the macroscopic world, but not to the world of subatomic particles. Newton's theories have been modified and extended by the development of quantum mechanics and the theory of relativity. This is also true of Darwin's theory. What is truly remarkable about evolution is how robust it has remained in light of the vast amount of knowledge we have accumulated since Darwin's time. This brings us to the second important aspect of scientific theories. They generate hypotheses or questions that can be tested. The theory of evolution generates two distinct, but overlapping questions. What is the evidence that evolution has occurred? This is the first question. The second question addresses the mechanisms of evolutionary change. Within these two broad areas of investigation Darwin's theory provided a far superior explanation than previous ones offered to three key questions. First, what was the cause of the extraordinary amount of diversity observed in nature? Second, how did the remarkable **adaptations** of organisms to their environment come about? Third, what was the basis for the *scala naturae* (natural ladder or **great chain of being**), that species could be arranged as part of a continuum that extended from the simplest to the most complex organisms? Making use of sophisticated tools to examine the fossil record, molecular sequence data of both **DNA** and protein to determine ancestry and investigate developmental processes, and a host of other techniques, has allowed scientists to build and expand on Darwin's basic insights and has provided a depth of understanding about this wonderful phenomenon of life. As will be explored more thoroughly in **Chapter 1**, evolution can address the objections that proponents of **intelligent design** (ID) raise, and more importantly, ID does not meet the criteria of what constitutes a scientific theory.

ORGANIZATION OF CHAPTERS

This book traces the history of evolutionary ideas beginning pre-Darwin and concluding with the latest research and controversies among working evolutionary biologists. With the book's historical approach, the reader learns not only about the facts of evolution, but also about the *process* of science. **Chapter 1** provides a brief history of the changing views of earth history pre-Darwin, setting the stage for the development of his theory. The perception that species were fixed and could not change was deeply rooted in Western civilization, shaped by both Greek and Judaic-Christian ideas. However, these beliefs were being compromised by a series of other ideas occurring over a long period of time that ultimately culminated in Darwin's theory of evolution. This included the discovery of **deep time** or geological time, and the changing meaning of fossils. A variety of theories were put forth to explain the origin and present-day conditions of the earth. The argument from design and its modern reincarnation, ID, are discussed. **Chapter 2** examines the life of Darwin and the development of his theory. It discusses the voyage of the *Beagle* and the other important influences on Darwin. The key ideas from each of the chapters of *The Origin* are presented. The reception of the book and the criticisms of it are examined. **Chapter 3** examines the maturation of Darwin's theory focusing on the importance of working out the laws of inheritance and the rise of population genetics in vindicating natural selection as the primary mechanism of evolution. In the 1940s what became known as the Modern Synthesis showed that findings from genetics, paleontology, systematics, and botany all provided overwhelming evidence in support of the theory. **Chapter 4** deals with the expansion of the synthesis. The elucidation of the structure of DNA provided evidence for evolution at the molecular level and gave rise to many new areas of investigation. Modern-day examples of natural selection in action are discussed as well as some crucial fossil organisms that were transitional between major groups. **Punctuated equilibrium** and evolutionary developmental biology (evo-devo) have not only presented new challenges to the Modern Synthesis, but also contributed to a more all-encompassing theory, as well as generating many additional, exciting areas of investigation. **Chapter 5** discusses human evolution. It begins with the debates over human evolution in Darwin's time and how he answered the most difficult problem: the evolution of the moral sense. The fossil evidence is also discussed. Molecular studies, including the **Out-of-Africa hypothesis** and the Genographic Project, are also providing evidence of the early history of our ancestors. **Chapter 6** explores the origin and early evolution of life. Recent findings suggest that before our current DNA-based life forms, life might have been **RNA** based. Molecular evidence suggests that three major divisions in life forms were established very early in life's history. The chapter also explores the importance of taking an evolutionary perspective in understanding disease, highlighting specific examples such as infectious disease including HIV as well as different chronic diseases. **Chapter 7** addresses evolution and humankind's future and explores evolutionary psychology, **evolutionary ethics**, the evolution of language, neurobiology, **mirror neurons**, and the development of empathy.

FURTHER READING

On the Origin of Species went through six editions and there have been numerous reprints. The year 2009 was the 150th anniversary of the book and Darwin's 200th birthday and a plethora of books were published on Darwin and evolution. Although all of Darwin's major works are available for free online, *On the Origin of Species: The Illustrated Edition*, edited by David Quammen (Sterling Press, 2008) is highly recommended and is the one cited in this book. It is beautifully illustrated, and contains an enormous amount of historical etchings, photographs, excerpts from Darwin's journals, and photographs of wildlife. For the history of the meaning of the word evolution see Thomas Huxley's 1878 essay "Evolution in Biology," in *Darwiniana,* 1893, pp. 187–226.

WEBSITES

National Center for Science Education http://ncse.com/evolution

Evolution Today: What is a Theory? bib.amnh.org/exhibitions/darwin/evolution/theory.php

1

THE DARWINIAN COSMOS

A CHANGE IN WORLD VIEW

Except for the Copernican Revolution no other development in science has caused such profound changes in cultural values – in how we view our place in the universe – as the Darwinian Revolution. In both cases fundamental aspects of the traditional Judaic-Christian world view were replaced by a new interpretation of the universe. The Copernican Revolution resulted in humans realizing that earth and, therefore, humans were no longer the center of the universe – no longer the center of a hierarchical cosmos stretching up to the perfect heavens. In breaking down the barrier between the perfect and unchanging heavens and the flawed earth, this new view of the universe meant that it was non-hierarchical and operated by fixed laws of dynamics.

In spite of this profound change, humans could still believe that they were spiritually unique and significant. Humans alone of God's creatures were moral beings, masters of a world that had been designed by the Creator to support them. Humans represented the peak in the "great chain of being" that united all things into a natural hierarchy. Surely no purely natural process could have led to the orderly system of life, especially to have created a thinking, reasoning, but most importantly a spiritual, moral being. Although in one sense the Copernican Revolution profoundly challenged humanity's place in the universe, in another way it left its position intact.

However, our place in the universe was compromised by another string of developments that was occurring over a long period of time that finally culminated in Darwin's theory of evolution.

THE ENLIGHTENMENT AND DISCOVERY OF DEEP TIME

The mechanical philosophy of Isaac Newton (1643–1727) and René Descartes (1596–1650) eliminated the need for the super-natural, except to create the basic laws that put the universe in motion. However, what was retained was the idea of design. The observed order in the universe was evidence for the existence of a creator, the master designer. The argument from design was an important theme that shaped many of the debates over evolution in Darwin's time and has reappeared today as intelligent design (ID). However, in the Enlightenment (1700s) the desire to explain the universe in mechanical/materialistic terms came increasingly to the fore, while at the same time there was less and less interest in reconciling the results of these investigations with the Bible.

Natural philosophers began thinking that the earth must be quite old, in part because findings in cosmology suggested that the universe might be infinite in both time and space. As Immanuel Kant (1728–1804) wrote, creation was never finished or complete and new galaxies and stars would evolve. Thus, the universe was no longer considered static, but was dynamic and evolving. This had profound implications for earth history as well. By the 1700s evidence was mounting that the earth itself had undergone profound changes. The discovery of extinct volcanoes along with other findings led to the realization that basalt was nothing but ancient lava, a remnant from ancient volcanic extrusions. Basalt was widespread and often found very deep in the earth's crust, which meant that it was quite old. At about the same time it was recognized that most geological strata were sedimentary deposits forming deep columns, sometimes more than 100,000 feet deep. It would take an enormous amount of time for that amount of sediment to be deposited. Furthermore, other processes were contributing to the changing of the earth's surface. The layers were eroded by water that often created deep valleys. Many layers had been folded and often so violently that they were completely turned over. Earthquakes and volcanoes also were constantly altering the earth's crust. Factions developed as to which of these forces were primary in shaping earth history, water (Neptunism) or fire (Volcanism), but the one point that everyone agreed with was that all these processes provided evidence that the earth must be far, far older than what was thought, based on a literal interpretation of the Bible. The Scottish geologist James Hutton (1726–97) argued that rather than these catastrophic processes, gradual processes of endlessly repeating cycles occurring over vast periods of time shaped the earth. He developed our modern concept of geological time that has become known as deep time.

An old earth had implications for the organic world as well. Originally the great chain of being was static and represented creation as it was first formed with species representing the links in the chain. **Extinction** could not occur nor could one species change into another. However, in the Enlightenment, temporalization of the chain occurred, i.e. the injection of time. Charles Bonnet (1720–93) suggested that the Creator had formed different kinds of germs destined to grow into different organisms in different periods of history. The chain was no longer a static plan. Rather, it had unfolded step by step through time to give the progression from the simplest forms at the bottom of the chain to the most complex at the top. Bonnet's scheme fit in with the growing desire to eliminate the need for miraculous interference with ongoing processes of nature. He attempted to deal with the growing interest in earth history that suggested geological catastrophes were the agents that prepared the way for each new population that would be adapted to the environmental conditions of its time. Georges-Louis Leclerc, Comte de Buffon (1707–88), introduced the idea of the "internal mold," which was characteristic of each species and maintained the species from generation to generation. However, he also suggested that the closely related forms, ranked in a Linnaean genus or family, were derived from a single original population that then became divided into separate groups through migration to different parts of the world. Influenced by the different climatic conditions, the ancestral population gradually changed its form over time. This was remarkably similar to our modern theory. Buffon also made a pioneering effort to study the geographical distribution of life and realized that this was a clue to the history of life. Nevertheless, he believed that species were fixed. True species were based on only a few internal molds and they did not change. Most Linnaean species were not considered true species in his scheme. Furthermore, the idea that the environment can act directly on the organism and change it and that those changes will be passed on to future generations was a far cry from Darwin's theory of natural selection. Nevertheless, all of these ideas undermined the creation story as they attempted to explain one of biggest challenges to Biblical literalism: the changing meaning and understanding of fossils.

THE MEANING OF FOSSILS

The ancients knew of fossils, but they had not used them to suggest either that the earth was millions of years old or that species changed through time. The original meaning of fossil simply meant "dug up" and included a range of objects such as natural crystals, mineral ores, as well as what we now define as fossils, i.e. something organic derived from once-living organisms. Furthermore, inorganic processes can often produce patterns in rocks that look surprisingly lifelike. Without understanding the process of fossilization, the origin of fossils was not obvious, and such an understanding did not come until much later. Robert Hooke (1635–1703) observed that the microscopic structure of fossil wood was very similar to that of charcoal or rotten wood. In 1665 in *Micrographia* he suggested that the fossil was derived from a once-living tree. Using the analogy of sealing wax, he also saw that organisms could leave impressions on suitable material, which in turn could serve as casts when material was introduced into these natural molds. Once he had a mechanism for explaining how fossilization could occur, Hooke concluded that fossils were the petrified remains of living organisms. He turned his attention to a special group of coil-shaped fossil shells known as ammonites. Some of the more loosely coiled shells were classified as "serpent stones" because they resembled a coiled snake. Hooke realized that both were a single group of shells. Niels Stensen, more commonly known as Steno (1638–86), had met Hooke and also became interested in fossils. When he examined a giant shark he noticed that the shark's teeth were quite similar to fossils referred to as "tongue stones" and he concluded that they were in actuality fossilized shark's teeth. If fossils were the remains of once-living organisms, Hooke recognized that they provided crucial pieces of evidence in understanding the history of the earth. Just as Roman coins or urns are clues to interpret a past civilization "fossils are the medals, urns, or monuments of nature."

However, fossils presented a serious challenge to the creation story. Many people were not convinced that fossils were indeed organic remains. Some people even suggested they were put on earth by God to test people's faith. Not only had alternative explanations been offered, but to accept them as being of organic origin also entailed providing an explanation to account for changes in physical geography that were implied by the *position* in which the fossils were found. Marine fossils were often found on the tops of hills, very far from the sea. Claiming that they had an organic origin involved radical changes in physical geography for which there was little good historical evidence. Various explanations were offered, trying to make these observations compatible with the Bible, such as invoking Noah's Flood, but none of them were entirely satisfactory.

By the nineteenth century with more and more fossils being discovered, it could no longer be denied that a large group of these dug-up objects were the remains of once-living organisms. Fossils moved to center stage in discussions over the age of the earth, playing a significant role in the debates over evolution. Fossils were problematic for two reasons. First, finding sea creatures embedded in particular strata implied that areas that were dry were under water at one time and thus, the earth was not fixed and static, but continually changing. Second, remains were being found that did not resemble any known living organism. What were these creatures; what had happened to them? Would God have created creatures only to let them die out? For theologians, this was a particularly vexing problem as it implied that the Creator had made a mistake and designed creatures that could not survive. Nevertheless, the researches of George Cuvier (1769–1832) demonstrated the reality of extinction, which seems obvious to us, but was not at the time (see **Figure 1.1**). Not only would extinction go against theological views, but naturalists also had their own objections. Although Hooke, Steno, and others claimed that fossilized shark teeth and ammonites belonged to species no longer living, critics of such a view rightly argued that just because no huge sharks had been collected in the Mediterranean and no ammonites found in the seas did not mean they did not exist. They could be so rare, or

Eon	Era	Period		Epoch	m.y.
Phanerozoic	Cenozoic	Quaternary		Holocene	
				Pleistocene	
					1.5
		Neogene		Pliocene	
				Miocene	
					23
		Paleogene		Oligocene	
				Eocene	
				Paleocene	
					65
	Mesozoic	Cretaceous			
		Jurassic			
		Triassic			
					250
	Paleozoic	Permian			
		Carboniferous	Pennsylvanian		
			Mississippian		
		Devonian			
		Silurian			
		Ordovician			
		Cambrian			
					540
Pre-Cambrian		Proterozoic			2500
		Archean			3900
		Hadean			4600

Figure 1.1 Strata and order of appearance of animal life upon the earth

exist in such faraway places, or at such great depths that they had not been discovered. Certainly such caution was well justified. In recent times organisms such as the coelacanth have been discovered representing a species thought to have long been extinct.

While fossils certainly were a challenge to the creation story, they by no means provided definitive support for Darwin's theory. The fossil record did not show one species gradually transforming into another. Rather it was full of gaps – species disappearing and new ones abruptly appearing. As Cuvier asked, were there species that existed that have been entirely destroyed, or have they been modified in their form, or have they simply been transported from one climate into another? In other words, had extinction, evolution, or migration occurred? While he thought migration might be a possibility for marine organisms, for the large terrestrial quadrupeds Cuvier claimed that the choices were either extinction or evolution. Cuvier argued against evolution for several reasons. His anatomic research suggested that organisms could be grouped into distinct types with no transitional organisms between them. Each species was a variant of a particular type, with the body parts harmoniously balanced. Any significant modification of any of the parts would upset the balance and make the individual unviable. Thus, he argued for the fixity of species on purely functional grounds. However, for purposes of this discussion, Cuvier believed that a theory claiming that fossil animals had been modified in their form over time, eventually giving rise to modern species, was a theory that essentially denied the reality of extinction. Thus, his anti-evolutionary position should not be construed as in favor of special creation, but rather as pro-extinction. Darwin was well aware that the fossil record was problematic for his theory of slow gradual change as will be discussed more fully in **Chapter 2**. Although extinction later became an important aspect of the mechanism of evolution, the issue of the gaps in the fossil record remains controversial. However, the debate is not about whether or not evolution occurred, but rather over what the pattern of the fossil record can tell us about the process of evolutionary change.

SETTING THE STAGE FOR DARWIN

As we can see, even by the 1700s, a great deal of evidence suggested that species were not fixed, and Darwin was not the first person to put forth the idea that species could change through time. His paternal grandfather Erasmus Darwin, a physician, naturalist, and a very colorful character put forth many of his ideas in poetry. In his work *Zoonomia* he argued that God had designed organisms to be self-improving through time. In their constant effort to face the challenges of the environment they developed new organs through time by a mechanism made famous by his contemporary Jean Baptiste Pierre Antoine de Monet, Chevalier de Lamarck (1744–1829): the inheritance of acquired characteristics. Lamarck is generally credited as the first major proponent of organic evolution. His theory consisted of three core ideas: (1) **spontaneous generation** of the simplest forms in both the plant and animal kingdom continually occurred; (2) organisms became increasingly complex over time; and (3) the particular circumstances to some extent thwarted this natural tendency toward increased complexity. This last idea was quite different than Darwin's. For Darwin, selection to the changing environment resulted in the branching that was key to generating diversity. For Lamarck, a series of distinct lines of evolution moved independently along the same scale of organization, progressing onward and upward. The chain of being would be forced into branches by the effects of different conditions – but this was of secondary importance to Lamarck. He did not believe that species had become extinct as the result of a global catastrophe. Rather they were transformed into other species, but the old forms were also continuously being replenished by the transformation of those lower down the chain. This explanation of organic change was possible because of the vast amount of time his geological views provided. As Darwin later argued, imperceptibly small changes accumulated over time producing all the different varieties of life observed in the organic world. However, Lamarck had no interest in the geographical distribution that would be key to the development of Darwin's theory. His mechanism of inheritance of acquired characteristics was fundamentally different than natural selection. Nevertheless, Lamarck's theory allowed an organism to adapt, to change, and it provided an explanation for how organisms became progressively more complex over time.

THE ARGUMENT FROM DESIGN

Seventeenth-century naturalists devoted increasing energy to describing animals and plants in great detail. The world of creation was far richer than anyone had imagined and naturalists were faced with the question of how to explain this diversity. Not only were explorers coming back from distant lands with previously unknown species, but also the development of the microscope revealed the existence of swarms of unknown tiny creatures. Several treatises provided a systematic classification of plants and animals. Classification is often the first step in developing a comprehensive theory. How we choose to divide up and order the world provides a framework for how we perceive it. However, classification alone did not explain how each species was intricately adapted to its way of life. John Ray (1627–1705), a first-rate naturalist as well as an ordained minister, argued in *The Wisdom of God Manifested in the Works of Creation* (1691) that the orderliness of nature, especially that observed in living organisms, was evidence of a Divine Creator. With his extensive and practical knowledge of adaptations he had observed in both the plant and animal kingdom, *The Wisdom of God* made a powerful case for the argument from design. Nevertheless, Descartes and other Enlightenment thinkers were systematically undermining the argument from design.

In 1802 the Anglican priest William Paley (1743–1805) reiterated the ideas of Ray, in *Natural Theology*. Nature gave overwhelming evidence for the unity of God that was seen in the "uniformity of plan observable in the universe." In his famous opening passage, Paley drew an analogy between the workings of nature and the workings of a watch. No one would believe that a watch, with its exquisite design, the detailed workings of its springs and gears all intricately fitted together, could have come about by a natural process. The existence of the watch implied the existence of a watchmaker. However, even the simplest organism was far more complex than the most complex watch. Thus, organisms, like the watch, could not have come about by a purely natural process, but rather must be the product of a divine watchmaker. The core of Paley's argument centered on adaptation. Example after example illustrated the remarkable adaptation of organisms to their environment, with every part of every organism designed for its function. The eye was an exquisite organ designed for sight. The human epiglottis was so perfectly designed that no alderman had ever choked at his feast. Even some species of insects were designed to look like dung to protect them from being eaten. The handiwork and divine benevolence of the Master Craftsman could be seen everywhere. God protected and looked after all his creatures, great and small.

Naturalism had great appeal to both religious and non-religious thinkers alike. Many religious thinkers, in fact, welcomed the developments in science, regarding them as an aid to faith. In theological circles, a line of thought was developing that became known as the higher criticism. The Bible was a historical document written by people and should be analyzed as such. Since the Bible was written by different people at different times in history, supposedly reflecting God's will, the interpretation of its meaning would always be problematic. **Natural theology** could serve as a mediator between different theological positions by offering independent proof of a God who had also revealed Himself in the person of Christ. Deists also liked the design argument because the more that could be known of God through rational inference, then the less dependent one would be on revelation and miracles to justify their faith. In addition, many people welcomed the challenges to orthodox religious belief and felt tremendous relief, no longer burdened by the Christian doctrine of original sin. However, the argument from design both furthered the belief in a Divine Creator and undermined Christianity at the same time. Relying on Nature for signs of God's benevolence was problematic. Nature was often cruel. Where was God in the slaughter that went on every day for survival? In the wild, it was eat or be eaten. An example that particularly upset nineteenth-century theologians was the ichneumon flies. Actually a group of wasps, many species followed a perversely cruel lifestyle. Although they were free-living adults, in the larval stages they were parasites feeding on other animals, usually caterpillars, but sometimes spiders or aphids as well. The adult female pierced the host and deposited her eggs within the caterpillar. When the eggs hatched, the larvae started eating from the inside. However, if the caterpillar died, it would immediately start to decay and be of no use to the larvae. Thus, the larvae ate the fat bodies and digestive organs first, keeping the caterpillar alive by preserving intact the essential heart and central nervous system. Finally, it killed its victim leaving behind the caterpillar's empty shell. Where was God's benevolence in this grisly tale? In spite of such problems, however, natural theology offered a powerful alternative for people who were finding it increasingly difficult to continue to believe in the tenets of traditional Christianity.

Darwin was thoroughly impressed with William Paley's ideas, and he saw first hand the evidence of nature's beautiful adaptations: from the differently shaped beaks of the Galapagos finches to the hooks and plumes of seeds that aid in their dispersal. As he wrote in his autobiography, he had always been "much struck by such adaptations, and until these could be explained it seemed to me almost useless to endeavour to prove by indirect evidence that species have been modified." As crucial as the idea of adaptation was to Darwin's thinking, in coming up with the principle of natural selection, ultimately he had to abandon the idea of *perfect* adaptation. Not only were organisms imperfectly adapted to their environment, but also many structures seemed to have no function whatsoever. Why did males have nipples if they didn't nurse their young? Why did cavefish have eyes that could not see? What use was our appendix? Eventually Darwin turned Paley's argument on its head. For Paley, the relationship between structure and function that resulted in the remarkable adaptations of organisms was powerful evidence for supernatural design. For Darwin, however, adaptation became a natural process by which organisms adjusted to a changing environment. There was no need for an intelligent designer.

INTELLIGENT DESIGN

The natural theologians of the nineteenth century and their followers were for the most part trying to keep up with scientific advances and at the same time search for a way to make religious ideas compatible with scientific ones. Many people were willing to give up a literal interpretation of the Bible, but they weren't about to become atheists. A lot of first-rate research was done, particularly in geology and paleontology in the service of natural theology. Darwin initially found the arguments in favor of natural theology quite compelling. He recognized that he needed to explain not just that species changed, but changed adaptively. The proponents of ID claim that this is a new theory, competing with Darwinian evolution; but virtually all the scientific arguments raised by ID are essentially reformulations of the argument from design. What might have been legitimate topics of debate in the nineteenth century are no longer so today. It is not a competing theory. The next several chapters will explain how Darwin addressed the objections, discussing candidly what he saw as weaknesses in his theory, and will also provide overwhelming evidence that has accumulated since Darwin's time in favor of even the most problematic aspects of his theory.

An important difference between the natural theologians of the past and the proponents of ID is ironically their motivation. Both groups interpret nature through the lens of religious belief, but the natural theologians really were looking for evidence of God in Nature. For them the natural law of the philosophers was merely a different terminology for God's law and reflected God's purposes. However, ID represents the latest in a series of attempts by Christian fundamentalists to have their particular belief system taught in the schools in the United States and has been spreading to other parts of the world as well. In the Dover, Pennsylvania, 2005 court case *Kitzmiller et al.* v. *Dover School District*, Judge Jones ruled ID failed to meet the criteria of what constitutes science on three different levels. First, science by definition is the investigation of the material world and thus does not invoke supernatural causation. Second, the argument of irreducible complexity, as will be explained below, does not hold up, and relies on the same flawed arguments that were used in support of creation science of the 1980s. Third, the scientific community has overwhelmingly refuted ID's negative attacks on evolution.

It is not just the poor science that is the most serious problem with ID. Answering ID's objections to Darwin's theory merely means that ID's science is incorrect. But many scientific ideas are eventually shown to be wrong. We no longer teach Ptolemy in an astronomy class, but that does not mean in its historical context Ptolemaic astronomy was not scientific. However, ID is not just outdated or incorrect science, but rather is unscientific. ID is not just disputing the theory of evolution, but represents an attack on naturalism, on the fundamental practice of science itself. Proponents of ID have done an excellent job in convincing many people that to accept evolution one must be an atheist, and it is true that some evolutionists such as Richard Dawkins have used evolution to promote an atheistic agenda. Yet many people accept evolution and still believe in God including biologist Ken Miller who testified in the Dover trial and Francis Collins, head of National Institutes of Health and who directed the United States government human genome project. Collins is firmly opposed to ID, but founded the BioLogos Foundation to "contribute to the public voice that represents the harmony of science and faith." While it is certainly true that evolution does conflict with particular tenets in the Bible such as the age of the earth, the fixity of species, and the descent of all humans from Adam and Eve, the theory of evolution does not take any position on the existence of God. However, evolution like any good scientific theory does not invoke the supernatural for explanation. Perhaps God did create the universe, but there is no way to investigate this question. As Darwin's "bulldog" Thomas Huxley (who coined the word agnostic to describe his own philosophical beliefs) wrote, the existence of God, the spiritual world and immortality lay outside the "limits of philosophical inquiry."

A key claim of ID is that many adaptations are "irreducibly complex" and could only be the result of design. Creationists cited the mammalian jaw, the vertebrate eye, and the bacterial flagellum as examples of structures that could not be products of natural selection acting on tiny variations. Yet all of these now have adequate scientific explanations. The eye was also a favorite example of the nineteenth-century natural theologians, and Darwin in *The Origin* seemed to agree, writing that to think it could be the product of natural selection was absurd. But he then went on to describe existing gradations of the eye. Some invertebrates have nothing more than nerve endings coated with photosensitive pigment. Some crustaceans have a double cornea, the inner one having facets, within each of which is a lens shaped swelling – while others have transparent cones coated by pigments. Darwin explained how natural selection acting on these various gradations of structure could eventually have produced an eye. Today we know that the lancelet, our closest living invertebrate relative, detects light with photosensitive cells that are wired up like the cells in the vertebrate retina. Other organisms have photosensitive spots on their skin, some that are essentially primitive lenses. Furthermore, the human eye is anything but an organ that has been designed intelligently. The photoreceptor cells of the retina have been put together backwards, aimed away from the light source. The optic nerve consists of a bundle of nerve fibers that carry the signals into the retina inside the eye and exit via a hole, creating a blind spot. The loose attachment of the retina to the underlying tissue makes it susceptible to becoming detached. Rather than ID, the eye reflects an organ that is built on what came before, the product of its history – a history that looks more like evolutionary tinkering than something that has been optimally designed. What is ID's explanation for poor design? It is due to the biblical fall of man.

ID asserts that evolution does not explain the gaps in the fossil record. This is a disingenuous argument. As will be explained more thoroughly in **Chapter 2**, there are many reasons for the gaps in the fossil record. Even within Darwin's lifetime many transitional organisms were discovered, bridging the gap between widely separate groups including between invertebrates and vertebrates and between flowering and non-flowering plants. Even the absolute distinction between plants and animals was breaking down with the discovery of simple life forms that had characteristics of both kingdoms. Now we have feathered dinosaurs, **Tiktaalik**, a lobed-finned fish that had many similar characteristics with **tetrapods** (four legged creatures that lived on land) and numerous fossils that represent transitional organisms between major groups. Today, what more powerful evidence could we have of common descent than the universality of the genetic code? The genetic instructions for making a particular amino acid are virtually the same whether in a mouse, an elephant, a human, or even a bacterium. This is why it is possible to take the **gene** that codes for human insulin, insert it in **bacteria**, and find the bacteria can "read" that gene and crank out millions of insulin molecules. Returning to the evolution of the eye, the Pax gene has been found to regulate the development of eyes in organisms as diverse as fruit flies, frogs, octopuses and humans. Thus, evidence for common descent has been found at life's deepest level, literally at the level of molecules.

Unlike evolution, ID is untestable and unfalsifiable. It has produced no experimental evidence in favor of design. Anything that does not have a complete scientific explanation is not evidence. As the distinguished paleontologist George Gaylord Simpson (1902–84) wrote, claiming that the absence of transitional fossils is evidence for creationism is equivalent to claiming that such fossils are always missing until they are found. Proponents of ID do not publish in peer-reviewed scientific journals, but rather in their own journals. All of their so-called scientific arguments have been refuted time and time again. However, the most serious criticism of ID is that the leaders behind the movement are intellectually dishonest. They continually quote people such as Stephen Gould out of context in support of their views. Gould and Niles Eldredge's theory of punctuated equilibrium asserted that the gaps in the fossil record were real and not just due to the imperfection of the fossil record. The theory engendered much controversy. It also revitalized paleontology and led to important new ideas that have extended evolutionary theory. To quote Gould in favor of their views is the height of hypocrisy.

The Discovery Institute has been the backbone for the fight to get religion in the schools. They have continually asserted that ID is pure science, but their true goal became clear when in 1999 an internal memo was leaked to the Internet, the infamous wedge document. Commenting on what they regarded as devastating social consequences of materialism, they claimed it needed to be cut off at its source, which was scientific materialism. "Our strategy is intended to function as a wedge. ... Design theory promises to reverse the stifling dominance of the materialistic worldview and to replace it with a science consonant with Christian and theistic convictions." As Judge Jones ruled, ID "cannot uncouple itself from its creationist, and thus religious, antecedents."

THE PROCESS OF SCIENCE

One of the marks of a good scientific theory is that it is capable of being tested, of being verified or falsified. Science does not represent "The Truth." Rather scientific theories are continually being modified as new evidence comes in. Many ideas proposed by scientists turn out to be wrong. Scientists will rarely refute their own hypotheses, but that doesn't matter because many other scientists working in the field will comment on the theories. Theories and "facts" must survive this period of testing and experimenting. Darwin's theory raised numerous questions. Was natural selection the primary mechanism of evolutionary change or are **mutation** and **Lamarckian mechanisms** also significant? Does the fossil record support a gradual or saltational (by jumps) view of evolutionary change? Can the mechanism of natural selection fully explain development or are other equally important mechanisms operating in turning an egg into an ostrich? All of these questions created controversy, but in doing so they stimulated new experiments, clarifying, and modifying, but most importantly validating and extending Darwin's basic ideas. Darwin's theory has been confirmed by literally millions of different bits of evidence. This is an example of how science works. One of the many unfortunate by-products of the religious fundamentalists' attempts to present scientific creationism and now ID as scientific theories competing with evolution is that it has sometimes stifled open discussion about the more legitimate sources of controversy within the scientific community. Nevertheless, controversy is alive and well among evolutionary biologists, but this should not be construed to mean the fundamental idea of evolution is under attack. It is not. Rather, controversy is the mark of a healthy scientific theory and in this regard evolution is exceedingly healthy, continuing to generate new and exciting insights about the natural world.

FURTHER READING

Bowler, P. (2009) *Evolution: The History of an Idea,* Berkeley: University of California Press.

Brooke, J. H. (1991) *Science and Religion: Some Historical Perspectives*, Cambridge: Cambridge University Press.

Miller, K. (2007) *Finding Darwin's God: A Scientist's Search for Common Ground between God and* Evolution, New York: Harper Perennial.

Rudwick, M. (1992) *Scenes from Deep Time,* Chicago: University of Chicago Press.

——(1972) *The Meaning of Fossils,* New York: Neale Watson Academic; repr. 1982, Chicago: University of Chicago Press.

WEBSITES

The Paleontology Portal bib.paleoportal.org/

The making of fossils bib.bbc.co.uk/sn/prehistoric_life/dinosaurs/making_fossils/makingfossils/index.shtml

Talk Reason bib.talkreason.org/

Nova Judgment Day: Intelligent Design on Trial bib.pbs.org/wgbh/nova/evolution/intelligent-design-trial.html

Argument from design: http://skepdic.com/design.html

2

THE DEVELOPMENT OF A THEORY

THE EARLY LIFE OF CHARLES DARWIN

Few figures in the history of science have received as much attention as Charles Darwin, so much so that the research on Darwin is referred to as the Darwin industry. Darwin was a prolific writer and has left us with an excellent record of the many important and varied influences that led to the development of his theory of evolution. He was born on 12 February 1809, the fifth of six children. His father Robert was a physician and his mother Susannah came from the Wedgwood family, known for its pottery and china, which made the family quite wealthy. He was a mediocre student, and his father once chided him, "You care for nothing but shooting, dogs, and rat-catching, and you will be a disgrace to yourself and all your family." However, he was quite curious, conducting chemistry experiments with his older brother Erasmus, and he showed a keen interest in nature, becoming an avid collector of all sorts of things – shells, seals, coins, and minerals. As was the family tradition, he was sent to University of Edinburgh to become a physician. He found the lectures "intolerably dull," and was nauseated by the operating theater. More interesting were the lectures by the zoologist Robert Grant (1793–1854), who took him to tide pools in search of sponges. Grant was a Lamarckian, and he thought that sponges might be one of the earliest life forms from which others had descended. Much to Charles' surprise, Grant told him he admired Darwin's grandfather who had espoused similar views to Lamarck. Darwin wrote in his autobiography that he was unimpressed with Lamarck. However, as will become clear, there are reasons to doubt Darwin's dismissal of Lamarck. Charles soon dropped out of medical school. His father was furious and worried that Charles would become one of the idle rich. Although not particularly religious Robert decided Charles should be ordained in the Church. Charles entered Christ's College in Cambridge in 1827. Such a calling had possibilities. As a country parson he would have enough leisure time to pursue his interest in natural history and indulge in his favorite sport of shooting game. However, just as in Edinburgh, he disliked most of his official studies, remarking "no one can more truly despise the old stereotyped stupid classical education than I do." Instead, he spent most of his time studying natural history and became a passionate collector of beetles. He soon made the acquaintance of John Henslow (1796–1861), a professor of botany and Reverend Adam Sedgwick (1785–1873), a professor of geology. Both men encouraged him to pursue a career in science. Sedgwick took him on a geological excursion in Wales in 1831 that provided him with excellent training for his later work. Even after the publication of *The Origin* and his later biological work Darwin always considered himself first and foremost a geologist. Darwin initially accepted Sedgwick's view of earth history that the earth had been shaped by a series of catastrophic episodes, events that had no counterpart in the present day. He would soon change his mind. While at Cambridge he also read Paley's *Natural Theology*, which made a profound impression on him. He had read Alexander von Humboldt's accounts of his travels and became excited about the possibility of studying natural history in the tropics.

THE VOYAGE OF HMS *BEAGLE*

Henslow had heard that the navy was sending a small ship, HMS *Beagle*, to chart the waters of South America. The captain, Robert FitzRoy, had created the position of ship's naturalist to describe the areas visited, in order to have a gentleman companion to relieve the monotony of the voyage; and Darwin was offered the job. Charles was thrilled, but his father was not. He thought that the voyage would be damaging to Charles' reputation as a clergyman, claiming that it was a wild scheme and would result in Charles never settling down. Fortunately for Charles, his uncle Josiah Wedgwood intervened. On 27 December 1831 Darwin set sail on a five-year voyage, which he described as "by far the most important event in my life," and which started him thinking about ideas that would profoundly affect Western civilization (see **Figure 2.1**).

Henslow had recommended that Darwin read the first volume of Charles Lyell's (1797–1895) *Principles of Geology* and Captain FitzRoy gave him a copy. Henslow had also cautioned him "on no account to accept the doctrine there espoused" – a warning not heeded. As Darwin later commented, "I always feel as if my books came half out of Lyell's brain." In contrast to the prevailing **catastrophism**, Lyell revived James Hutton's **uniformitarianism**, arguing that the same forces that shaped geological formations in the past were in operation today. Furthermore, these processes – such as erosion, volcanoes and earthquakes – were of the same intensity as those operating in the past and, thus, the present was the key to understanding the past. Uniformitarianism was more than just a theory about earth history. It provided a research methodology for investigating the past. The young Darwin had ample opportunity to put this precept into practice. As he explored the volcanic rock at St Jago of the Cape Verde Islands he recognized that the lava had flowed out from under water, baking the coral and shells. Later, forces must have lifted the rock up to the sea's surface, but then lowered and lifted it up again. This must have happened relatively recently since a band of fossil shells embedded in the cliffs were the same as present-day organisms found on the island. As he wrote in his autobiography, St Jago "showed me clearly the superiority of Lyell's manner of treating geology, compared to that of any other author." While in South America Darwin made several extensive excursions inland and in 1835 he observed the terrible effects of a major earthquake in Chile. This devastating upheaval had permanently raised the level of some land around Concepción by as much as 10 feet. Darwin reasoned that earthquakes acting over hundreds of thousands of years could explain the vast number of fossil seashells found at Valparaiso at elevations of over 12,000 feet in the Andes. Over long periods of time such

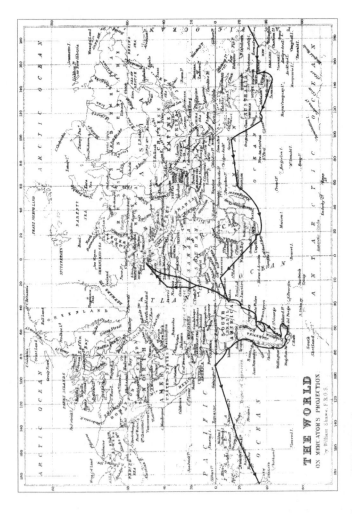

Figure 2.1 Voyage of HMS *Beagle*

movements would produce large-scale effects such as the building of mountain ranges.

Already Darwin's keen analytical nature showed itself as he did not accept all of Lyell's ideas, but rather used them to develop his own. One purpose of the *Beagle* voyage was to survey all the coral reefs of the Indian Ocean, which the ship crossed towards the end of its voyage. Lyell had written that coral reefs were only formed on the tops of submerged volcanic craters. However, Darwin put forth a different theory that turned out to be the correct explanation. Darwin had observed that the reefs always seemed to form perfect circles around islands or even around just water. As a result of having confirmed it with his own observations, Darwin accepted Lyell's view that the Andes were rising. If this was true, then other parts of the earth must be sinking, for example in the Indian Ocean. Darwin suggested that corals might grow in shallow waters around newly formed islands and along mainland coasts. As the land began to sink so would the corals, but new corals could grow on them forming a reef. The old coral that was completely cut off from sunlight would die, but one could find the skeletal remains of it. An island might completely disappear, but the reef would still survive near the ocean surface. As the *Beagle* surveyed different reefs, it found every stage that Darwin had suggested. In the Cocos Islands, the seaward side of the reef had a sharp drop off, and at the bottom the coral was dead, but provided a scaffold for the live coral, just as Darwin predicted. Nevertheless, Lyell's idea of a dynamic changing earth, being shaped by the same forces in the past that were operating today, informed Darwin's thinking and this applied not just to the inorganic world, but the organic one as well.

As the *Beagle* continued its exploration Darwin continued to observe and collect, sending numerous specimens back to England. Some of his observations made him begin to doubt the idea of special creation and the fixity of species. In Punta Alta of Patagonia he discovered many fossils of huge extinct animals such as the *Glyptodon* that looked very similar to our present-day armadillos. Why would the Creator make similar forms allowing others to go extinct? Argentina was also the home of two distinct species of rhea that had slightly overlapping ranges. Why would God think it necessary to create two different species that were found in similar habitats? Much has been made of the importance of the Galapagos to Darwin's thinking, but the full significance of the Galapagos only became apparent later. Nevertheless, Darwin collected extensively from several of the islands and it soon became apparent to him that the islands had been colonized from the mainland of South America.

THE GALAPAGOS ISLANDS

The Galapagos are often referred to as a living lab of evolution, a group of relatively young volcanic islands about 600 miles off the coast of Ecuador. They had been known as the Islas Encantadas or Enchanted Islands on the sea charts. Enchanted as in bewitched since ships had trouble navigating the different islands due to powerful currents in the straits. Although most of the islands had no fresh water source and many had large areas that were essentially barren and covered by black lava, the islands teamed with life. An astonishing array of plants and animals representing both tropic and arctic creatures lived side by side as a result of warm ocean currents from the west and cold ones from the south. Penguins, seals and sea lions mingled with tropical birds including flamingos, a wide variety of reptiles, and cacti. Darwin was both fascinated and repulsed by the two species of iguanas. On Chatham Island (now San Cristóbal) he encountered the sea iguana. "The black lava rocks on the beach are frequented by large most disgusting clumsy lizards." On the island of Albemarle (now Isabela) Darwin observed a second iguana that was entirely land based. "Like their brothers … they are ugly animals. … They have a singularly stupid appearance. … In their movements they are lazy and half torpid." Darwin had heard about the tortoises, and initially accepted the prevailing view that the tortoises had been brought there by the Spanish as a source of food for sailors and were not native to the islands. He and the rest of the crew happily ate them, Darwin writing that they made delicious soup and not realizing that he was literally eating evidence that would later be useful to him. Close to the end of the *Beagle*'s six-week visit, the British director of a small penal colony, Nicholas Lawson of Charles Island or Floreana (now Santa Maria), told Darwin that he could tell which island a particular giant tortoise came from just by looking at its shell. He pointed to the numerous flower pots made from carapaces of the tortoises, each exhibiting a distinct pattern. Each island had it own distinct species, some more than one, and all were endemic to the islands. Due to the extensive slaughtering of tortoises by humans, a couple of species were already extinct and several others were close to extinction. Until meeting with Lawson, Darwin had failed to note the differences between the different island tortoises, commenting only on their slowness while riding one. He had also merged his specimens from the various islands.

Darwin initially might have missed the significance of the tortoises, but he had paid attention to the mockingbirds, noting that different varieties existed on each of the different islands. However, he did not know whether they were distinct species or merely different varieties of the same species. Nevertheless, they appeared to be similar, but distinct from the mainland species and from each other. This was also true for the iguanas. Darwin had thrown a sea iguana into the ocean several times, but it continually swam back to the shore (confirming how stupid he thought it was since if it stayed in the sea it could have escaped his bothering it). It acted in every way like a land iguana, only going to sea to feed. After he dissected several of them he found they were vegetarians, just like their land-based relatives, but feeding totally on seaweed.

Darwin had also observed the differently shaped beaks of what are now referred to as Darwin's finches, each species adapted for its unique lifestyle and diet. Some lived mainly on the ground and ate only seeds from cacti or other plants while others were found in the trees and ate insects or leaves. However, he did not realize that they all belonged to the same group (finches), but instead thought they belonged to several different groups, calling some grosbeaks, some finches, and some wrens. He put the cactus-eating ones into the category of "Icterus" a group that included orioles and blackbirds. As with the tortoises, he also had not labeled which island a particular specimen came from. It was not until he was back in England and consulted with the ornithologist John Gould who sorted out the different birds and informed him that they were all finches that he recognized the full implications of his collection. Furthermore, the variations seen in the beaks could also be seen as evidence for the argument from design. Captain FitzRoy wrote in his diary, "This appears to be one of those admirable provisions of Infinite Wisdom by which each created thing is adapted to the place for

which it was intended." Darwin at this time was not an evolutionist, writing in his journal "It will be very interesting to find
from future comparison to what district or 'centre of creation' the
organized beings of this archipelago must be attached." Nevertheless,
the flora and fauna certainly were suggestive that as the islands
became colonized, the island inhabitants diverged from their ancestors
on the mainland, eventually becoming distinct species.

Darwin may have spent most of his time observing the natural
history of the many places the *Beagle* visited, but this trip would
play an important role in his views about human evolution as well.
Both his grandfathers had been leading abolitionists and he was
shocked to find the prevalence of slavery in Brazil. When the ship
docked in Bahia he saw first hand the brutality and cruelty of slavery. He watched in horror as slaves in shackles were beaten and
children and spouses separated from one another as they were sold
in the slave market. Aboard the *Beagle* were three Tierra del Fuegians,
Jemmy Button, York Minster, and Fuegia Basket. Brought to
England by missionaries, they had been living in London for the past
four years, but were being returned to their home. In their short
time in England, they had become quite Anglicized in both manner
and dress: Jemmy in his fine London clothes and Fuegia in her
English bonnet. Darwin was continually amazed by many little
traits of character that showed how similar their minds were to
Europeans. They were a stark contrast to members of their own
tribe that Darwin saw on the shores of Tierra del Fuego. This was
the first time Darwin observed "wild men" in their native habitat
and he was truly shocked.

> I shall never forget how savage & wild one group was. ... They were
> absolutely naked & with long streaming hair, springing from the ground &
> waving their arms around their heads, they sent forth most hideous
> yells. Their appearance was so strange that it was scarcely like that of
> earthly inhabitants.
>
> (Darwin, 19 December 1832, *The Voyage
> of the Beagle* [2001: 194])

Could these naked barbarians, their bodies coated with paint, and
their often-unintelligible gestures really belong to the same species
as the Europeans? Darwin shared the belief that was common at the

time that Western culture represented the pinnacle of social evolution and that other groups were inferior. Yet Darwin realized that Jemmy undoubtedly had behaved in just the same manner as the "miserable savages whom we first met here." The contrast between the Fuegians on board and those in their native land made Darwin realize both the tremendous potential for change and improvement and the tenuous state of civilization. He thought that the differences among humans were even greater than between wild and domesticated animals, because humans were capable of greater improvement. In less than four years Jemmy had gone from a stage of savagery to someone who made jokes and polished his shoes. However, the "savage" behavior of the Fuegians would be something he would ponder for many years to come.

Darwin may have been shocked and repulsed by the native Fuegians, but he did not for a moment accept the theory of **polygenesis**, that proposed that different races actually represented different species. All human beings, no matter how diverse they were today, ultimately were derived from the same common stock. The amazing plasticity of human beings as shown by the contrast between the native Fuegians and the ones aboard ship would be crucial to his later formulation of a theory of evolution. Cruelty and brutishness as well as kindness and sympathy were all part of the human condition. If the gap between the civilized and savage races could be bridged, which was greater than that between domestic and wild animals, this would provide the foundation for his assertion that no unbridgeable gap existed between animals and humankind. He wanted to discredit the theory of polygenesis that many used as a quasi-scientific argument to justify slavery, but this did not mean that he thought the so-called primitive races were equal to Europeans. Darwin would later think that the present-day primitive races provided a window into the past, exhibiting behavior that was undoubtedly quite similar to that of ancestral primitive races. This would suggest a chain of continuity from an ape-like ancestor, to primitive human ancestor, to present-day humans.

As Darwin continued his observations around the globe, he became more and more convinced that species were not specially created. The geographical distribution of organisms, particularly what he had observed on the various islands, and the geological formations all suggested to him that species had changed over time.

However, a crucial question remained: How did such change occur? He did not think that Lamarckian mechanisms of change – the action of the environment and the will of the organisms – provided an adequate explanation of how organisms were so exquisitely adapted to their habits of life. William Paley's ideas were still prominent in his thinking as he saw first hand the evidence of nature's beautiful adaptations, from penguins whose wings had changed to enable them to essentially fly underwater, to cacti whose leaves had been modified to minimize the loss of water. However, he had also seen organisms that were not so perfectly adapted. He saw woodpeckers in a land with no trees, geese with webbed feet who never went near the water. Why would the Creator place animals in places where they did not seem to belong?

During the voyage, Darwin received the second volume of Lyell's *Principles of Geology*. *The Principles,* however, was not just a book on geology and the second volume dealt entirely with species. Lyell saw that the series of geological strata and the sequence of forms in the fossil record were different aspects of the same problem. Were species real and permanent, or were they capable of being indefinitely modified over a long period of time? Lyell provided a detailed critique of Lamarck's theory of transmutation and concluded that the evidence did not support Lamarck's views. However, Lyell admitted it was often difficult to see the boundaries between species and varieties, as there were greater differences between some varieties than between some distinct species. In actuality, *The Principles* gave a mixed message about the transformation of species. Herbert Spencer (1820–1903) after reading Lyell's refutation of Lamarck's views became a Lamarckian and developed his own view of evolution before Darwin. "Lyell's arguments produced the opposite effect of that intended." It was Spencer who actually used the word evolution rather than transmutation and who coined the phrase "survival of the fittest" that Darwin later adopted. Darwin also took a different message from *The Principles*. Lyell's discussion of the distribution, extinction, and creation of species, of competition and variation, was just the type of evidence that Darwin would later use to support his own theory of evolution by natural selection. He would take Lyell's idea of slow gradual change in the inorganic world and apply it to the organic world.

THE BUILDING OF A THEORY

The *Beagle* returned to England on 2 October 1836. Darwin devoted the next several years to writing up his observations that he eventually published in 1839 as *The Journal of the Researches into the Geology and Natural History of the Countries Visited During the Voyage of HMS Beagle Round the World*. It was an enormous success, and later became known simply as the *Voyage of the Beagle*, and remains one of the greatest travelogues ever written. In 1837 Darwin also began a series of private notebooks in which he started to systematically assemble ideas and evidence in favor of transmutation. The project soon expanded to include not only the origins of plants and animals, but humans as well. He wrote to people living abroad such as missionaries to give him their impressions of native people. He visited zoos, observing carefully the behavior of animals. Seeing the expression on an orang-utan that reminded him of the expression seen in human babies he made a note "Man from Monkeys?" He went back and examined his specimens from the Galapagos more carefully. It was only now with the help of Gould that he recognized that the finches could be used as powerful evidence in favor of common descent.

> The remaining land-birds form a most singular group of finches. Related to each other in the structure of their beaks, short tails, form of body, and plumage. ... There are thirteen species ... all these species are peculiar to this archipelago ... The most curious fact is the perfect gradation of the beaks, in the different species ... Seeing this gradation and diversity of structure of one small, intimately related group of birds, one might really fancy that from an original paucity of birds in this archipelago, one species had been taken and modified for different ends.
>
> (Darwin, *Voyage* [2001: 339]; see Figure 2.2)

However, the most important evidence that Darwin would use in support of common descent came not from field observations, but rather from embryology. Darwin had come of age at a truly exciting time for biology. Voyages such as those of the *Beagle* had increased dramatically and naturalists were bringing back a cornucopia of organisms to be dissected and classified in an attempt to comprehend the natural history of the planet. At the same time

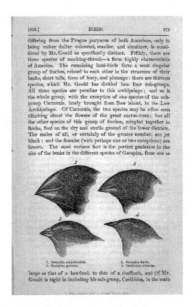

Figure 2.2 Darwin's finches

improved methods of microscopy made investigations in the laboratory possible that had not been so earlier. Pre-Darwinian naturalists had long been interested in developing a classificatory scheme that reflected the natural grouping of organisms based on the similarity of structure. According to Goethe (1749–1832) and the *Naturphilosophen* or transcendental morphologists, the essence of an organism was an independent ideal form or type, while living organisms represented variants and departures from this underlying essence. Comparative anatomists and morphologists were interested in finding this basic plan or type that could be discerned at different taxonomic levels and that could be used to explain the overall organization and functioning of an organism. This morphological concept of type was ubiquitous in the nineteenth century, with the *Naturphilosophen* its most auspicious advocates. As Thomas Huxley wrote, "The doctrine that every natural group is organized after a definite archetype, [is] a doctrine which seems to me as important for zoology as the theory of definite proportions for chemistry." However, Huxley was not interested in the transcendental morphologists' abstract or imaginary ideas upon which animal forms were modeled. In his own research Huxley was guided by the type concept of Karl Ernst von Baer (1792–1876). By examining the embryonic development of a variety of organisms von Baer concluded that organisms could be grouped into four major types: the mollusc, articulate, radiate, and vertebrate. Von Baer believed these types were distinct and argued against transmutation. However, he acknowledged that a certain amount of change could occur within types. Furthermore, all animal forms had undergone some kind of differentiation and the further back one traced **development**, the more similar widely different animals appeared. He asked "Are not all animals essentially similar at the commencement of their development – have they not all a common primary form?" He even suggested that at the earliest stages the embryos of invertebrates and vertebrates would be indistinguishable. For von Baer the "history of development is the history of a gradually increasing differentiation of that which was at first homogeneous." His ideas were summed up in his four famous laws of development: (1) the general characters of a large group of animals appear earlier in their embryos than the more special characters; (2) from the most general forms the less general are developed, until finally the most special arise; (3) every embryo of a given animal form, instead of passing through other forms, rather becomes separated from them; and (4) fundamentally therefore, the embryo of a higher animal form is never identical to any other animal form, but only to its embryo. In the last two laws von Baer wanted to distinguish his views from those of **recapitulation**, that the ancestral stages of the adult were repeated in the embryonic stages of its descendants forming a linear hierarchy. Étienne Geoffroy St Hilaire (1772–1844) used the idea of recapitulation to advocate transmutation. He maintained that the embryo of a higher organism passed through all the stages of the animal kingdom, adding more structures, becoming more complex, and in doing so, Geoffroy argued that the whole history of life was replayed in the developing embryo. Von Baer disagreed. An individual species within a given type might be highly developed with regard to one organ system and quite primitive in all others. Thus it was not possible to arrange organisms in a linear chain of increasing perfection. The *scala naturae* simply did not accurately represent the natural order.

George Cuvier agreed with von Baer. He also grouped animals into four basic types or *embranchements*, but he found those types by looking at the comparative anatomy of adults. Rather than a structural approach, Cuvier emphasized function. He claimed that organisms only shared basic plans because they carried out similar interrelated functions. His classification was based on a hierarchy of anatomical characteristics, with the nervous system being the most important. He found four basic types of nervous systems. His famous principle of the correlation of parts reflected his belief that every organ in the body was related and dependent on every other organ in order to maintain the functional integrity of the organism as a whole. It was not possible to modify one organ without modifying others and still maintain harmony. This principle explained the lack of transitional forms between various groups, particularly between the *embranchements*. For Cuvier the *embranchement* was not an abstract taxonomic category, but represented a natural system of classification that also meant that species were fixed. At the same time Cuvier's extensive work on fossils also demonstrated the abrupt appearance and disappearance of groups and organisms. Extinction was real. Where did new organisms come from?

Several prominent researchers saw parallels between embryonic development and the fossil record. William Carpenter borrowed von Baer's idea of an undifferentiated germ becoming more specialized as development proceeded and applied it to the fossil record. In *Principles of Physiology* (1853), he suggested that the fossil record showed a progression from a generalized archetype to a more specialized form. Richard Owen, a prominent anatomist, came to the same conclusion as Carpenter, resulting in a minor priority dispute over virtually identical theories. The paleontologist Louis Agassiz (1807–73) claimed that the successive creations of life on the earth passed through phases of development **analogous** to those through which the embryo passes during its growth. While all of these men argued that the fossilized forms of extinct species were recapitulated in present embryos, von Baer was clear that resemblances would be to ancestral embryonic forms, not adult ones. However, they all agreed that the divergence observed both in fetal development and in the fossil record seemed to be part of a wider developmental plan. They used development and the fossil record to specifically argue against evolution. Furthermore, whether one adopted the structural approach of von Baer or the functional approach of Cuvier, the type concept advocated by both men seemed to provide convincing evidence that species were fixed.

Once again Darwin's genius becomes apparent as he absorbs the ideas of many different thinkers, building on their findings, but coming to different conclusions. Darwin acknowledged Owen's expertise in comparative anatomy and asked him to examine his fossil mammalian specimens. Geoffroy might have been an advocate of transmutation, whereas Cuvier and von Baer argued against it; yet Darwin would draw more on the ideas of Cuvier and especially von Baer as he developed his own ideas. Darwin recognized that the concept of type provided powerful evidence in favor of his theory. Darwin's ancient progenitors were the archetypes of various animal species. He believed that in these ancient animals the adult form and the embryo were similar. The archetype was in some degree embryonic and therefore, capable of undergoing further development. This was the explanation for Darwin as to why embryos resembled ancient fossil forms. For von Baer, these resemblances were the necessary consequence of moving from a common starting point by a single process of increasing specialization. For Darwin, the pattern in the fossil record was the result of descent from a common ancestor with divergence and increasing specialization occurring over time. Although the variations from the general archetype were inherited, they usually did not make their appearance until late in development, while the embryonic stages remained unchanged (see Figure 2.3).

Darwin was convinced that organisms did change through time. He found the evidence from comparative anatomy and embryology along with his field observations such as that of the finches and mockingbirds compelling. He drew in his notebook a diagram of a tree with branches showing how some species became extinct while others diverged, giving rise to other branches. There was no linear scale; as he wrote, "[i]t is absurd to think of one animal being higher than another." However, he was still lacking a mechanism for how this species change came about. Quite early on Darwin thought that the familiar practice of plant and animal breeding might offer clues to the origin of species. Ultimately domesticated plants and animals were derived from wild ancestors in a process involving descent with modification. The breeders continually

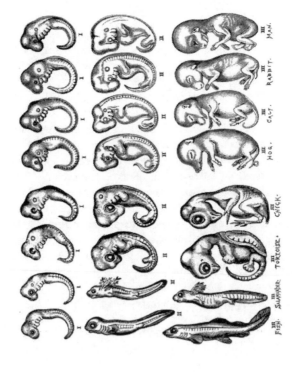

Figure 2.3 Embryological evidence of common descent

selected individuals with desirable traits and then bred those individuals among themselves. All the different varieties of dogs, from an Irish wolfhound to a little terrier, had descended from common stock, the result of selective breeding. Indulging in a hobby common to many English gentlemen, Darwin became a bit of an expert pigeon breeder and realized that given enough time and patience artificial selection could cause astonishing results. Examining their skeletons demonstrated the amazing amount of divergence that could be achieved. If these varieties had been found in the wild they would have been classified as separate species. Yet all these varieties had descended from the common rock dove. Could a similar process be occurring in the wild?

In October of 1838, Darwin happened to "read for amusement" Thomas Malthus's (1766–1834) essay *On the Principle of Population.* Malthus argued that a universal tendency existed for human populations to greatly exceed their available food supplies, which resulted in a continual "struggle for existence." Urban overcrowding, intense competition for jobs, poverty, disease, all provided evidence for Malthus's principle of population. A visit to the East End of London confirmed that life for its poor inhabitants was quite literally a struggle for existence. Malthus provided the final piece to the puzzle of species change for Darwin, because he immediately realized that this struggle was not confined to human populations. He knew from his own experiments that far more individuals were born than survived to reproduce. Who survived and who perished? Was it just a matter of chance? To the casual viewer the individual seedlings in an oak forest or the offspring in a population of sparrows might look identical, but Darwin had observed that the amount of variation within populations was essentially limitless. He reasoned that useful variations would tend to be preserved and unfavorable ones would be destroyed in the ongoing continual struggle for survival. Those favorable variations would accumulate through the generations in the same way as desirable traits accumulated in domestic populations that were the product of selective breeding. Eventually a new species would be formed. With the analogy of artificial selection in mind Darwin called this process natural selection. Natural selection not only provided a mechanism for species change, but it explained how species change *adaptively* in the continual struggle for existence.

Darwin knew that his theory would cause an uproar, particularly the idea that humans might have descended from an ape-like creature, but he continued to gather evidence. In 1842 he wrote a sketch outlining his ideas, showing it to no one. However, he continued to develop his thoughts and expanded the essay. By 1844 the essay was 164 pages long. He left instructions to his wife Emma and £400 to have it published posthumously along with names of suitable editors if something should happen to him. But finally, he had to discuss his ideas with someone. He wrote his good friend and colleague Joseph Hooker (1817–1911), a botanist who had examined his specimens from the *Beagle*, "I am almost convinced (quite contrary to the opinion I started out with) that species are not (it is like confessing a murder) immutable. ... I think I have found a simple way by which species become exquisitely adapted to various ends."

Hooker was quite impressed with Darwin's idea, although he still had his doubts about various aspects of it. Darwin began to consider publishing his essay, still worried about how the general public would receive it. As it turned out, shortly after he finished the essay, Victorians became exposed to many of his ideas with the anonymous publication of *Vestiges of the Natural History of Creation*. The anonymous author was Robert Chambers, a Scottish journalist who argued that the Creator by working according to natural law created simple forms of life that progressively changed, eventually giving rise to organisms such as human beings with a rich and complex mental life. The book was an outstanding success, in spite of being quite controversial. It sold thousands of copies and went through numerous editions. Darwin read the *Vestiges* carefully and paid close attention to the reaction it engendered. He thought that the author's "geology strikes me as bad, and his zoology far worse." But to himself, he had to acknowledge that the anonymous author had used many of the same kinds of evidence – embryology, the fossil record, classification, and comparative anatomy – that he had gathered for his own theory of species change through time. Darwin had much more in common with Mr Vestiges than he was willing to admit in public. Although people such as Owen, Lyell, and Sedgwick all attacked the *Vestiges* supposedly on the basis of its faulty reading of the fossil record and distortion of embryology, this was not their real objection. Rather, they recognized that the

Vestiges presented an explicitly evolutionary account of the history of life even if it was couched in the language of natural theology. This progressive account had profound implications for the nature of humans and their origins. Darwin did not publish his essay. He knew he had to tighten up his arguments and continue to collect evidence if he was going to win over his colleagues.

Darwin began what became an eight-year study of barnacles. It had only recently been recognized that barnacles were a type of crustacean. Starting with a specimen he collected in Chile, he eventually examined thousands of specimens and decided it would be valuable to examine the whole subclass since so little was known about them. He eventually wrote a 1,000-page treatise on barnacles and the subclass *Cirripedia* that remains the most authoritative account of the group. Surprisingly, the barnacles only received a few pages in *The Origin*. Although his barnacle research showed how they could have diversified, resulting in many different species, their classification became what would be predicted by his theory of evolution rather than a source of insight into the development of it.

By the mid-1850s Darwin had taken several people into his confidence. Lyell had known possibly as early as 1837 that he had begun to doubt the fixity of species, but it was not until 1856 that Darwin appeared to have fully explained his idea of natural selection. With Darwin as the catalyst Hooker, Lyell, Carpenter, Huxley, and others in the Philosophy Club debated the idea of species change. Lyell wrote in his journal that "the belief in species as permanent fixed & invariable … is growing fainter." Darwin was encouraged to publish his ideas and began working on the "big book" that was to be titled *Natural Selection*. Darwin had been in correspondence with a younger naturalist, Alfred Russel Wallace (1823–1913). Wallace's own research would force Darwin to come "out of the closet" about his ideas.

Wallace is one of the more interesting men associated with Darwin. In addition to advocating a theory of evolution, he also believed in phrenology and mesmerism and later became a committed spiritualist. Socially progressive, he also advocated the abolition of private property. Like Darwin, Wallace had traveled and made extensive observations around the globe. After spending two years in South America and then returning home for two years, he left in 1854 for the Malay Archipelago. He lived there for eight years and gathered over 125,000 specimens. In organizing them he pioneered the study of the geographical distribution of plants and animals, which later provided crucial evidence to advance his theory of evolution by natural selection. Wallace noticed a division within the flora and fauna of the Australasian islands, which followed a line of demarcation that today is still known as the Wallace Line. In 1855 he wrote a brilliant essay, "On the Law Which Has Introduced the Introduction of New Species," that drew on his observations not only in the Malay Archipelago, but from South America as well. He had noticed that many species on the opposite sides of the rivers in South America were closely related, but not the same. Yet physical conditions were virtually identical. The geographical distribution of organisms on the Galapagos Islands had made a profound impression on him, just as it had on Darwin. On the theory of special creation one would have expected the organisms on the islands to be identical to one another since their environments were the same. They should have been significantly different from the mainland species since the environments were so different. Yet each island had species unique to itself and from the mainland species, but nevertheless, they were similar in form. How did this happen? Wallace reasoned, as had Darwin, that the islands must have been initially populated by species from the mainland through winds and ocean currents. Sufficient time had passed that the original mainland species had died out and only the modified prototypes remained. Thus new species always came into existence at the same time and place of closely allied species.

Wallace continued to gather data, all of which reinforced what he had observed on the Galapagos and in South America. In the Malay Archipelago, the organisms found in New Guinea and on the Aru Islands were completely different from the western islands such as Borneo. However, the two countries were virtually identical in terms of climate and physical conditions. In contrast, physical conditions could not be more different between Australia and New Guinea, but the two faunas were strikingly similar. Wallace concluded that something other than the law of special creation must be responsible for both the structure and distribution of organisms. Like Darwin, Wallace also searched for a mechanism of evolutionary change. While ill with malaria on the island of Ternate, he was reading Malthus, and just as with Darwin, Malthus supplied the key insight for Wallace to independently come up with the law of natural selection.

Wallace had been corresponding with Darwin for years, but in 1858 he sent Darwin a letter along with his paper entitled "On the Tendency of Varieties to Depart Indefinitely from the Original Type," in which he outlined virtually the identical theory of natural selection. Darwin was devastated and wrote to Lyell, "I never saw a more striking coincidence; if Wallace had my MS sketch written out in 1842, he could not have made a better short abstract!" Lyell and Hooker did not want Darwin to lose priority since he had outlined these very ideas many years earlier. They arranged for extracts from Darwin's unpublished writings and Wallace's paper to be read before the Linnaean Society. Wallace stayed on for several more years in the Malay Archipelago, while Darwin frantically worked on a shorter version of his big book and in 1859 published *On the Origin of Species by means of Natural Selection or, The Preservation of Favoured Races in the Struggle for Life*.

THE PUBLICATION OF *ON THE ORIGIN OF SPECIES*

On the Origin of Species was published on 24 November 1859; the entire run to bookshops sold out in the first day. In addition to advocating a theory of evolution it contained a vast compendium of facts: facts of comparative embryology and anatomy, the latest findings in geology, paleontology, and biogeography that Darwin had been accumulating for over twenty years. He wove all this information into a compelling tale of how species slowly changed through time by his mechanism of natural selection. As Darwin asserted in the final chapter, the whole volume was "one long argument." The structure and organization of the book reflected an underlying logic that was powerful and persuasive. In the introduction he told the reader that the central problem of evolution was adaptation. He recognized that it was critical to explain adaptation as well as change if he was going to challenge the arguments of the natural theologians. In chapters one and two he documented the widespread variation that existed both under domestication and in nature. From the random variations that existed in nature, breeders artificially selected organisms with desirable traits and selectively bred them, creating enormous diversity. In the wild, nature became the selector. As species became adapted to local conditions, many varieties and races were created and taxonomists often disagreed as to whether something should be classified as a variety or a species. Darwin argued that these varieties could be considered to be incipient species, and that the term species was somewhat arbitrary. Chapter three, entitled "The Struggle for Existence," provided numerous examples of the struggle, which resulted from the fact that all species tended to reproduce far more offspring than could be supported by the environment. One particularly dramatic example was elephants. Elephants had the slowest reproduction rate of known animals, but Darwin calculated that after 500 years 15 million elephants would be alive, descended from a single pair if nothing checked their numbers. Individuals competed for food, for habitat, and for mates. Thus competition was most keen among individuals within species and between closely related species. Something must keep the population in check. Darwin had carefully prepared the reader for chapter four in which he explained the mechanism of natural selection. In this constant struggle, Darwin asked the reader, wouldn't "individuals having any advantage however slight over others ... have the best chance of surviving and of procreating their kind? ... any variation on the least degree injurious would be rigidly destroyed. This preservation of favourable variations and the rejection of injurious variations I call Natural Selection."

Chapter five continued to build the case for natural selection by examining the laws of variation based on the observations of many different organisms. Animals of the same species adapted to living in a colder climate by having thicker fur than those in a temperate region. Was this adaptation the result of the direct action of the severe climate, "conditions of life," or was it due to natural selection? This was an extremely difficult distinction to make, but he noted that often the same varieties were reproduced over varied climates and also different varieties were found under the same conditions. He concluded that the trait for thicker coats must be inherited, and that the effect of the environment on traits was relatively small. Furthermore, the potential for a trait to be expressed was not lost even after innumerable generations of it not being expressed. He recognized that the germ line contained a tremendous pool of variation for natural selection to act on. Darwin was hampered by his lack of information on the laws of inheritance and had to build his case based only on the visual characteristics of the organism. However, description marks the first phase of a natural science and Darwin's careful observations provided many insights on the laws of variation. In chapter six, "Difficulties of the Theory," Darwin addressed many of the objections that he anticipated would be brought against his theory. First he discussed the lack of intermediate forms between species. Rather than a problem, this would be predicted from an evolutionary process of branching and divergence. The intermediate and less adapted forms would continually be exterminated resulting in the gaps between present-day species. Extinction and natural selection went hand in hand. What about organs of extreme perfection? Here Darwin confronts the strongest argument of the natural theologians – how did organisms become so well adapted to their environment? What use would intermediate stages be? What good is half a wing? How could a non-flying mammal evolve into a bat when such an organism would presumably have limbs that were not well adapted either to fly or walk? Yet flying squirrels were just such organisms with their ability to glide from tree to tree. A classic example of perfect adaptation brought forth by the theologians was the human eye. As mentioned in chapter two, Darwin found many organisms that had eyes with varying degrees of complexity that were nevertheless useful to the organism. In Darwin's obsession with adaptation, the key to explaining it was giving up the idea of perfect adaptation. The more he looked the more he found that nature was filled with many structures that were "good enough" and far from perfect. Once again, this was exactly what would be predicted by natural selection, which had to build on what was inherited rather than designing something from scratch.

Chapter seven dealt with **instinct**. Just as body parts evolved so did behavior, which was just as critical to survival as having well-adapted body parts. Natural selection acting on very tiny variations could result in the development of highly complex behavior that could be extremely beneficial to the organism. His prize example of such a behavior was the building of hive cells by the honeybee. The honeycomb consisted of hexagonal-shaped cells. Mathematically this was the most efficient design. It resulted in the biggest storage space, using the least amount of wax. How could this have come about? The honeybee certainly doesn't know geometry, and built perfect combs purely on instinct. However, there were other species of bees that showed gradations in their cell-building, from spherical ones with much wax between them to eventually more and more tightly packed hexagonal cells. A swarm that had wasted the least amount of honey in the secretion of wax would have the best chance of succeeding and passing on this newly acquired instinct to new swarms. Bees along with various other social insects presented another problem that appeared to be potentially fatal to Darwin's theory. They often have an entire group of sterile females. Since they did not reproduce, how could such a trait have evolved? In explaining this Darwin essentially advocated group-level selection, writing "selection may be applied to the family, as well as to the individual." Darwin observed that in some groups the neuters became highly specialized among themselves, having quite different structures and instincts. There were working and soldier ants having very different jaw structures. Some worker ants never left the nest and were fed by others who had an extended abdomen secreting a honey-like substance. Once again careful observation revealed a gradation of structure among individuals; however, the vast majority appeared to have structures that were best suited for a particular function. This division of labor resulted in increased efficiency for the community as a whole. Although the trait may have become correlated with sterility, it benefited the fertile males and females and so the community flourished, passing on the traits. Group selection has been a highly contentious issue among modern evolutionary biologists that will be addressed in greater detail in the final chapter. In chapter eight Darwin addressed the problem of hybrid sterility. Species were defined largely by their inability to interbreed with other species. Even if offspring were produced, such as a cross between a horse and a donkey, the resulting mule was sterile. This was crucial if species were to be kept distinct and it seemed plausible that sterility under Darwin's theory should be selected for. Darwin showed that gradation existed between varieties within species that freely crossed and ones that were partially sterile. Some species had varieties that were totally incapable of interbreeding, while some individuals that were considered to be members of distinct species when crossed were capable of producing fertile offspring. Darwin maintained that the distinction between varieties and species was somewhat arbitrary. Varieties could be considered incipient species and if proper conditions occurred they might eventually become distinct species. Sterility was not selected for, but was an incidental by-product of acquired differences.

Today the fossil record is always cited as support for evolution. However, Darwin was well aware of the problems that the fossil record presented for his gradualist scheme. "Geology assuredly does not reveal any such finely graduated organic chain, and this perhaps is the most obvious and serious objection which can be urged against the theory." In chapters nine and ten Darwin amassed an enormous amount of evidence to convince his readers that while the fossil record might not be cited in support of his theory, at least it wasn't against it. The globe had only just begun to be explored systematically for fossils. Only those organisms with hard parts were likely to be fossilized. Particular conditions had to be met before something would become fossilized. He borrowed an analogy from Lyell who said that reading the geological record was like reading a book where most of the pages were missing and only a few words were on each page. In short, the fossil record was woefully imperfect. Darwin argued that the gaps in the fossil record were due to the irregular process of fossilization, competitive exclusion, and migration into new areas. Whether an organism was actually preserved or not depended on so many different factors that the fossil record represented a quite incomplete chronicle of the history of life. Moreover, transitional organisms by definition were transitional. Thus their numbers were likely to be small, their geographic range would be limited as well, making it extremely unlikely that they would be fossilized. The organisms that appeared in the record had already diverged significantly from a common ancestor, resulting in a record with many breaks. This was true for the gaps between present-day organisms as well. For example, birds appeared to be totally distinct from other vertebrate animals, but Darwin believed that the ancestors of birds were connected to the ancestors of other vertebrate classes. In chapters eleven and twelve Darwin discussed many of his observations from the *Beagle* voyage regarding the geographic distribution of organisms to powerfully argue that evolution by natural selection was much more plausible than the theory of special creation to explain the history of life on earth.

In chapter thirteen Darwin presented what he considered the strongest evidence for evolution, and that was the evidence used in classification. The morphological type concept was crucial to that endeavor as it provided an organizing principle that could be used to explain the overall structure and functioning of an organism.

> What can be more curious than that the hand of a man, formed for grasping, that of a mole for digging, the leg of the horse, the paddle of the porpoise, and the wing of the bat, should all be constructed on the same pattern, and should include the same bones, in the same relative positions?

In describing similarities, most naturalists defined affinity as a strong similarity in important characters, with analogy being a peculiar similarity between species not related by affinity. However, such a distinction was vague and confusing. Richard Owen clarified the distinction between the two by defining an analogue as "a part or organ in one animal which has the same function as another part or organ in a different animal" and a homologue or affinity as "the same organ in different animals under every variety of form and function." Tracing patterns of development as exemplified in the work of von Baer was key to making this distinction. Taxonomists in their search for affinities or homologies were trying to distinguish superficial similarities from more meaningful ones, although they did not realize that the order they were searching for was due to descent from a common ancestor. However, they were sensitive to the types of evidence that made for good classification and Darwin drew heavily on such evidence to support his theory. His theory explained *why* organisms could be arranged in the way they were, but the facts of that arrangement were well in place pre-*Origin*.

In the final chapter Darwin summarized all the arguments in support of his theory. His one long argument explained both change *and* adaptation. Since "natural selection worked solely for the benefit of each individual, both physical and mental endowments will tend to progress towards perfection." Darwin ended by asking the reader to imagine an entangled bank that was teaming with life:

> ... plants of many kinds, with birds singing on bushes, with various insects flitting about and worms crawling thought the damp earth ...

these elaborately constructed forms, so different from each other and dependent on each other in some complex a manner have all been produced by the laws acting around us.

THE RECEPTION OF *ON THE ORIGIN OF SPECIES*

After reading *The Origin* Huxley exclaimed, "How stupid not to have thought of it before." Dubbing himself Darwin's bulldog, he told Darwin that "he was prepared to go to the stake if necessary" against the enemies of evolution. Nevertheless, Huxley raised many issues that were problematic for the theory that continued to re-surface throughout the twentieth and twenty-first centuries. Examining Huxley's objections provides a means of demonstrating how powerful and robust the theory of evolution has turned out to be. Based on the work of Cuvier, of von Baer and his own research, Huxley thought species were fixed. Organisms appeared to be grouped into distinct types with no transitions between them. But unlike them, Huxley recognized that the evidence also sup-ported descent from a common ancestor. Darwin's theory, never-theless, presented a dilemma for Huxley. How could one reconcile evolution with the concept of distinct types? Furthermore, the fossil record did not show one species gradually evolving into a different one. He thought evolution by **saltation** or jumps seemed to better fit the facts of development and the fossil record. On the eve of the publication of *The Origin*, he cautioned Darwin, "You have loaded yourself with an unnecessary difficulty in adopting 'Natura non facit saltum' so unreservedly" (Nature does not make jumps). Such a view also suggested that natural selection might be able to cause the formation of well-marked varieties, but lacked the power to create true species.

Huxley eventually abandoned his saltational views as a result of increasing evidence of transitional organisms. In 1861 a very pri-mitive reptilian-like bird fossil was discovered, ***Archaeopteryx*** (see **Figure 2.4**). However, it was still classified as a bird. Thus, it couldn't really be the connecting link between birds and reptiles. Huxley suggested that dinosaurs were the connecting link between birds and reptiles. Some dinosaurs were remarkably bird-like in a variety of ways – for example the structure of the pelvis in

Fig. 702.

Archaeopteryx lithographica H. v. Meyer. Skelet im britischen Museum von Langenaltheim bei Solnhofen. ca. ⅓ nat. Gr. (nach Owen). Links ist der Hinterfuss, rechts der Vorderfuss besonders dargestellt.

Figure 2.4 Archaeopteryx

Megalosaurus and *Iguanodon*. Particular bones in the dorking fowl if found in a fossil state would be indistinguishable from those of a dinosaur. Moreover, if it were somehow possible to enlarge and fossilize the hindquarters of a half-hatched chicken, it would be classified as a dinosaur. Evidence continued to build in support of this idea, with the discovery of more and more bird-like dinosaurs, and in the 1990s feathered dinosaurs were discovered in China – a stunning validation of Huxley's suggestion and also of the idea of gradual change.

For Huxley, however, the most persuasive evidence in favor of gradual evolutionary change was a series of fossil horses discovered in North America. In the third and final lecture on evolution Huxley gave in the United States in 1876 (the first one was attended by two thousand people and printed in its entirety in the *New York Times*), he claimed that the succession of forms was "exactly and precisely that which could have been predicted from a knowledge of the principles of evolution," i.e. forms gradually would become better adapted to their environment, becoming more specialized over time. In a detailed and somewhat technical discussion of the changes in the structure of the legs and teeth, he showed that the more ancient the horse was the more it resembled the generalized mammalian form. He even predicted what the characteristics would look like in a horse from the Cretaceous. Two months after he gave the lecture, such a form was discovered from the lowest Eocene deposits of the west (see Figure 2.5).

In spite of what proponents of ID claim, even within Darwin's lifetime transitional organisms continued to turn up, bridging the gap between widely separate groups, including between invertebrates and vertebrates and between flowering and non-flowering plants. Even the absolute distinction between plants and animals was breaking down with the discovery of simple life forms that had characteristics of both kingdoms. Nevertheless, saltation has continued to resurface, receiving its most serious attention with the theory of punctuated equilibrium, which will be addressed in **Chapter 4**. Today, it is accepted that the fossil record exhibits both kinds of patterns, gradual and punctuated change.

Descent with modification was quite quickly accepted because it provided the theoretical underpinnings to classification; however, natural selection was not. By 1874 Huxley was convinced that species gradually changed, but he remained skeptical of natural selection, causing Darwin to refer to him as the "Objector General" on the matter. Huxley maintained that the evidence did not yet exist that demonstrated natural section was capable of creating good physiological species incapable of interbreeding, and not merely well-marked varieties such as the various breeds of dogs or pigeons. He agreed with Darwin that it could be difficult to determine what

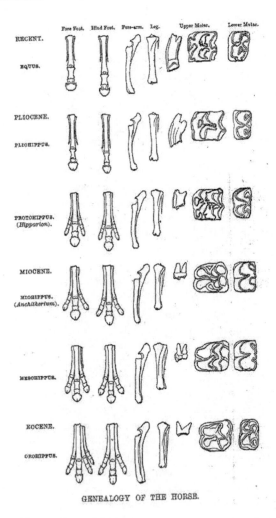

GENEALOGY OF THE HORSE.

Figure 2.5 Marsh's genealogy of the horse

was a variety and what was a species. He recognized that breeding experiments often gave inconclusive results. Darwin took Huxley's objections quite seriously. He realized that if he could demonstrate hybrid sterility was an acquired or *selected* character, natural selection would be in a much stronger position. He enlisted the aid of various breeders and continued to do experiments himself in an effort to convince Huxley that the sterility problem was not insurmountable. The young horticulturist John Scott used selective breeding to successfully create varieties of *Primula* (primrose) which when crossed produced offspring that were completely sterile. Huxley's criteria of creating a physiological species had finally been met. Much to Darwin's frustration Huxley was still not convinced. Although Darwin agreed with Huxley that hybrid sterility was an important measure of speciation, the opposite argument could be made as well. The results of hybridization experiments were often contradictory. The sterility or fertility of crosses appeared to bear no relation to the structural similarities or differences of the members of any two groups. The fact that offspring from crosses between different varieties were often partially sterile while crosses between individuals that botanists claimed were distinct species sometimes resulted in fertile offspring was evidence that hybrid sterility was *not* a good criterion for defining species. If this was the case, there was no reason that sterility factors should be selected for. In addition, the inability to interbreed cannot be applied to organisms that reproduce asexually. Further research convinced Darwin that his original view was correct: sterility was an incidental result of differences in the reproductive systems of the parent species.

Natural selection, however, was not fully accepted as the primary mechanism of evolutionary change until the next century with the development of population genetics. The most controversial aspect of Darwin's theory was the implications for human origins and he chose not to address the issue in *The Origin*, writing only, "Light will be thrown on the origin of man and his history." Human evolution will be discussed in **Chapter 5**.

FURTHER READING

Browne, J. (1995) *Charles Darwin, Voyaging,* Princeton: Princeton University Press.
——(2003) *The Power of Place,* Princeton: Princeton University Press.
Darwin, C. ([1839] 2001) *The Voyage of the Beagle,* New York: The Modern Library.
Fichman, M. (2004) *An Elusive Victorian: The Evolution of Alfred Russel Wallace,* Chicago: University of Chicago Press.
Lyons, S. (1999) *Thomas Henry Huxley: The Evolution of a Scientist,* Amherst, NY: Prometheus Books.

Lyell, C. ([1830–33] 1991) *Principles of Geology: being an inquiry how far the former changes of the earth's surface are referable to causes now in operation,* 3 vols, repr. Chicago: University of Chicago Press.

Ospovot, D. (1981) *The Development of Darwin's Theory: Natural History, Natural Theology, and Natural Selection, 1838–1839,* Cambridge: Cambridge University Press.

WEBSITES

The Complete Work of Charles Darwin Online http://darwin-online.org.uk/

Darwin, American Museum of Natural History bib.amnh.org/exhibitions/darwin/

Evolution: Darwin bib.pbs.org/wgbh/evolution/darwin/index.html

The Huxley File http://aleph0.clarku.edu/huxley/

Geological Time Machine, from University of California Museum of Paleontology bib.ucmp.berkeley.edu/help/timeform.html

In Darwin's Footsteps bib.sulloway.org/DarwinFilm.mpg

3

THE MATURATION OF A THEORY

A THEORY OF INHERITANCE

The previous chapter showed that Darwin's theory of evolution had several different components and they met with varying degrees of acceptance. Although descent with modification was quite quickly accepted, natural selection was not. Sir J. F. W. Herschel referred to natural selection as the "law of higgledy-piggledy," which expressed many people's repugnance to what seemed to be a random undirected process being responsible for the great pageantry of life. Thomas Huxley, in spite of his being the foremost supporter and defender of Darwin's theory, voiced a more substantive objection. He asked whether selection, either natural or artificial, had the power to create new species as opposed to well-marked varieties. Part of the problem was that although Darwin documented how widespread variation was in nature, he did not know the source of that variation. Variation was the raw material for natural selection, but the variation must also be inherited. Darwin had his own theory of inheritance that he called pangenesis. He noted that since the buds of a tree and the polypi of a coral could have a somewhat independent existence as well as a communal life he thought that organisms were composed of numerous semi-independent units. He also had observed that if one cut up the flatworm planarian, the parts could regenerate a whole organism. Thus, the potential for making the whole organism must be present in all parts of the body, not just the germ cells. Polyps could throw off buds that also formed a whole organism. Darwin thought that all the cells had small invisible particles that he named gemmules or pangenes and were responsible for particular traits. These gemmules could be modified by the environment and they were free to circulate in the body. They were thrown off by the different cells and accumulated in the reproductive organs. This would then explain how acquired characteristics could be passed on to the next generation as well as the reversion to ancestral characters. Pangenesis never had much of a following, but it did encourage research exploring the link between inheritance and evolution. Darwin's cousin Francis Galton (1822–1911) transfused the blood between differently colored pure breeds of rabbits. If pangenesis was true then the rabbits that received the transfusion should have offspring with a different coat color. Even after many generations this never happened. Nevertheless, many traits seemed to exhibit what looked like Lamarckian inheritance. By the sixth edition of *The Origin* Darwin relied on Lamarck's idea of use and disuse much more heavily than in the first. However, natural selection remained his primary mechanism that drove evolution.

Galton may have discredited pangenesis, but he shared Darwin's view that variation must be inherited through material particles. He also thought that they remained unchanged through many generations. He started studying whole populations, applying new statistical methods, including regression and correlation analysis. He showed that traits were not lost, nor were they modified. Variation and inheritance were two aspects of the same phenomenon. Inheritance was the means by which the variation was preserved in the population. In his book *Hereditary Genius* Galton argued that accomplished men who came from good families were more likely to have superior offspring, i.e. talent and intelligence was largely inherited. He coined the word **eugenics** from the Greek meaning good or well born, advocating selective breeding to improve the qualities of a population. Although eugenics has quite a horrible legacy, its ideas being used to justify sterilization practices and anti-immigrant fever in the first part of the twentieth century as well as being a cornerstone of the Nazi program, Galton's work was important as it showed that heredity could be studied separately from reproduction and this would be crucial to working out the laws of inheritance. At the same time a mechanism was still needed for how the traits were passed on from generation to generation, something that neither he nor Darwin showed much interest in. The answer to these questions would eventually come from work in cell microscopy.

LAMARCKIAN INHERITANCE AND THE CONTINUITY OF THE GERM PLASM

August Weismann (1834–1914) was the person most responsible for discrediting Lamarckian inheritance with his theory of the **germ plasm**, building on key ideas that had been advanced as a result of improved methods in microscopy. In 1838–39 Matthias Schleiden and Theodor Schwann proposed their cell theory. They showed that all organisms, whether plants or animals were made up of cells. Each cell had an outer membrane, the enclosed contents, and a central area called the kernel or nucleus. By carefully observing the process of cell division, Rudolph Virchow argued that cells only arose from the division of pre-existing cells. Other researchers showed that the nucleus was formed from a pre-existing nucleus during cell division and that the egg and sperm were each single cells that were called gametes. The nuclei from the gametes fused during fertilization and this suggested that the nucleus was the source of the hereditary material.

Weismann argued that the germ cells must also arise from pre-existing cells, passing on some chemical substance in the nucleus that contained the information to direct the development of a complete organism of the same species. He reasoned that the germ plasm must have discrete determinants for the various traits of the organism. By the 1880s it was shown that before division the nuclear material formed distinct chromosomes. By a complicated process later called **mitosis**, the chromosomes were duplicated and then divided equally into two new cells. If this was so, Weismann reasoned, the gametes must contain only half the hereditary material in order that upon fertilization the normal chromosome number would be restored to allow development to proceed by mitosis. It was later confirmed that gametes were produced by a duplication of chromosomes just as in mitosis, but followed by two divisions rather than one. This resulted in four gametes, each with half the number of chromosomes in regular cells. This process, known as **meiosis**, was further confirmation that the chromosomes contained the hereditary material (see **Figure 3.1**). Since they were sequestered in the reproductive organs, the germ plasm was uninfluenced by the growth of the rest of the organism. Like Galton, Weismann also did an experiment to prove his idea. He cut off the tails of mice and bred them. Generation after generation of mice who had their tails cut off never produced mice with shorter tails. The modifications that were brought about by use or disuse or action of the environment did not affect the germ line. Instead, the variation that was observed in the **genotypes** was the result of two processes: first the shuffling and recombination of the various determinants, as a result of sexual reproduction; and second, sometimes accidental errors were introduced in the copying of the hereditary material. Variation was thus undirected. From this Weismann argued that natural selection was what drove the adaptive changes that were observed in evolution.

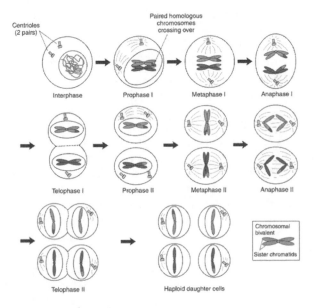

Figure 3.1 The stages of meiosis

In this period we see the separation of heredity and development into distinct disciplines. Previously they were tightly linked, resulting in a major debate over how development occurred. Was it epigenesis or preformation? Weismann's ideas seemed to present a way out of this dilemma. In its most extreme form preformation claimed that inside the egg was a complete little miniature of the organism. It merely grows, i.e. all the information was already there and in early manuscripts one can find drawings of homunculi – little tiny miniature humans within the egg. Inside one homunculus was another and inside that another, like a Russian doll. An obvious problem with this idea even with a literal interpretation of the Bible was that it implied that Eve contained the whole future of the human race inside her. By the nineteenth century this debate had been pretty much resolved in favor of epigenesis or an unfolding. The organism developed cumulatively as increasingly complex structures formed from the initially more or less homogenous material of the fertilized egg. Every new embryonic formation was building on what came before. However, epigenesis was not without its problems. How did the organism know how it was to grow? Why did the frog egg turn into a frog and not a cat? The fertilized egg must not just be some homogenous blob. It must contain some plan right from the beginning that tells it to become a frog, not a cow or an elephant. Thus one could argue that the preformationists were not entirely wrong. The contrast was not as clear-cut as what the early debates seemed to imply. We may laugh at the little homunculus today, but in a sense Weismann's idea is based on the concept of preformation. Weismann believed that the germ cells contained all the primary constituents to direct the growth of the individual. We now know that the instructions are contained in DNA. Development, however, has turned out to be a much more difficult problem to fully understand than the laws of inheritance, and its importance for evolutionary theory was essentially ignored until relatively recently. The incorporation of development into evolution will be examined in **Chapter 4**. Furthermore, we now know that the hereditary material is not completely shielded from environmental effects, which also explains why examples of what looked like Lamarckian inheritance continued to be found. Alternations to the DNA such as methylation, that do not involve changes in sequence can profoundly alter gene function and therefore phenotype. Such changes can also be inherited. Understanding these **epigenetic** changes is an active area of research, particularly as it relates to health and disease.

MENDEL'S PEAS

Unbeknownst to Darwin the laws of inheritance were being worked out by the Austrian monk Gregor Mendel (1822–84). Mendel was also interested in the problem of speciation and thought that by hybridizing existing forms new species might be produced. He began breeding experiments with the garden pea. He identified seven characters that existed as clear-cut alternatives such as round or wrinkled seed coat, green or yellow seeds, white or violet flowers, etc. When Mendel crossed two true-breeding plants of each type, in the first generation (F1) they all resembled only one of the parental type. For instance, between green and yellow seeds, the first generation was all green. He described green as the dominant trait while the one that did not appear was recessive. However, it had not been lost. In the F2 generation, he found the ratio was three green to one yellow. The **recessive trait** was only masked. Carrying on to the third generation by self-fertilization, he found that those plants with the recessive trait, for example wrinkled seeds, bred true, giving rise to only wrinkled seeds. One third of the dominant trait round also bred true. The remaining two thirds of the round seeds gave rise to both round and wrinkled in a 3:1 ratio (see **Figure 3.2**). Mendel did a large number of experiments, crossing and self-fertilizing literally thousands of plants. He concluded that the recessive element was masked by the dominant one, but was still available to the next generation for transmission. By doing several different crosses with different traits he also concluded that each pair of elements assorted independently. Although Mendel was familiar with Darwin's work, the reverse does not appear to be the case. Mendel worked in relative obscurity and his ideas had virtually no impact until the 1900s when his work was rediscovered and replicated by two different researchers: Hugo De Vries (1848–1935) and Carl Correns (1864–1933). With the rediscovery of Mendel's papers the principles of the animal and plant breeders were reinterpreted in Mendelian terms. However,

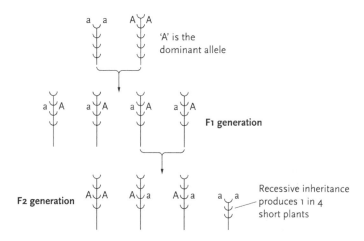

Figure 3.2 A monohybrid cross
Source: Adapted from *Genetics for Healthcare Professionals*, Figure 19, p. 59

Mendelian genetics was initially used against Darwin's theory of selection acting on small variations.

HUGO DE VRIES, WILLIAM BATESON AND MUTATION THEORY

Mendel is credited with being the father of genetics but it was William Bateson (1861–1926) who first coined the term "genetics" in 1906. Bateson agreed with Darwin that variation was the raw material of evolution and decided that the best way to study evolution was to study variation. He thought there were two kinds: discontinuous and continuous. The latter was what was widely observed in nature and was responsible for the slight individual differences observed in a species, such as plant height, leaf size. Animals often showed gradation in the color of their fur and also varied in their shape and size. It was these small variations that Darwin argued were what natural selection acted on, producing change slowly and gradually. However, Bateson adopted Huxley's initial view that new species were created by sudden jumps. Bateson, working in the field, identified several species that had distinct forms with no intermediates. He concluded that speciation was the product of discontinuous variation and started breeding experiments to understand the laws of inheritance of these discrete discontinuous variations. De Vries also was studying the laws of inheritance of discrete traits and used Darwin's term pangenes for the units responsible for them. Independently he discovered the same general rules of inheritance that Mendel had worked out forty years earlier. Bateson introduced several terms to clarify the laws that Mendel and de Vries had discovered. **Segregation** referred to the separation of the hereditary units in meiosis and was responsible for the definite ratios. The units that segregated he called **alleles**. If they were the same when recombined in the zygote, for example both alleles coded for round seeds, this was referred to as being **homozygous**. If they differed from one another, one round and one wrinkled, he called this **heterozygous**. The laws were important, but for de Vries they still did not offer any insight into how new species actually arose. He began intensive breeding experiments with the evening primrose. He cultivated two plants that were quite distinct from the normal type found in the wild. They bred true, but also threw out new forms that continued to breed true and were so distinct that he justified calling them new species. Several new forms appeared in a single step. De Vries called these new discontinuous variations mutations. These were inherited, while the other small variations were due to environmental fluctuations and were not. It was not until later that it was realized that the evening primrose was an unusual hybrid species and the mutations were not in fact what de Vries thought they were. Rather, we now know that mutations are changes in the DNA that often, but not always, give rise to an altered genotype and **phenotype**.

In this period the idea of mutation was melded with Mendelian inheritance. De Vries claimed that mutations arose at once, creating new forms that followed Mendel's laws. Natural selection only weeded out the mutations that were not advantageous. Mutation was the driving force of evolution rather than natural selection. Bateson agreed and claimed that Darwin's view that evolution occurred by the accumulation of tiny variations was false. For these men neither natural selection nor adaptation played any significant role in the origin of new species. At the turn of the century the Darwinians were caught in a controversy defending natural selection against neo-Lamarckian ideas on the one hand and Mendelian ideas on the other.

THE RISE OF POPULATION GENETICS

In spite of the popularity of the mutation theory, most naturalists working in the field saw small variations and adaptation everywhere. Biometricans Karl Pearson (1857–1936) and W. R. Weldon pioneered a statistical approach to analyzing these traits that showed continuous variation such as in plant height. Along with the naturalists, they thought new species arising by saltation seemed extremely unlikely. Mendel's laws applied to discontinuous variation, discrete traits such as the round or wrinkled seeds with nothing in between, but did not seem to explain the continuous variation they observed and which they thought was crucial to how evolution occurred. One of the best examples of natural selection acting in the wild was the phenomenon of mimicry. Henry Bates, who had explored South America with Wallace, had noticed that some species of butterflies from quite different families looked so similar that it was virtually impossible to tell them apart when flying. Yet the mimetic species was often divided into distinct geographical races that were linked by intermediate forms. Bates thought that mimicry was an adaptation brought about to protect the species from predators, as he had noticed that the butterfly that was being mimicked had an unpleasant smell and thought it was probably unpalatable. Insectivorous animals would eat the individuals that looked the least like the unpleasant tasting butterfly, eventually resulting in a variety that looked virtually identical to the species that was unpalatable. Bates had observed several intermediate stages, and in light of Darwin's theory argued that the key to such an adaptation was "numerous small steps of natural variation and selection." Mimicry is extremely widespread in nature and has often evolved to enable species to escape predators. Caterpillars that look like twigs, various insects looking like leaves or bark, all blend into their environment to escape detection. Alternatively, many species from insects to frogs to snakes are brightly colored, but such coloration mimics a poisonous species that in turn has evolved bright colors as a warning. Darwin had also shown in his study of orchids that mimicry served another important function: reproduction. Some species of orchids had evolved structures that looked like female wasps or bees. The male arrives, attempts to mate with the flower and in the process pollinates the flower with pollen brought from another orchid, as well as picking up pollen from the current flower.

In spite of these many wonderful examples of adaptation, some naturalists also reiterated a serious question. How could natural selection create novel traits? Selection could not push a population beyond the limits of the variation that was in the parent population. The solution to both these problems was to unravel the genetics of continuous variation. Danish biologist Wilhelm Johannsen (1857–1927) established several distinct pure lines of the garden bean which tended to self-fertilize and thus were largely homozygous. By careful statistical analysis he showed that each line of beans varied continuously in size over a certain range. The variation in offspring was virtually identical from generation to generation and remained constant regardless of what size bean he grew the plants from. As a result of this work he introduced several new terms. He used the term "**gene**" for the pangene of de Vries and made the fundamental distinction between genotype and phenotype. The genotype referred to all the genes in the fertilized zygote. The phenotype was what an organism looked like as a result of the interaction between genes and the environment. The environment was responsible for the variation he observed in his pure lines. Herman Nilsson-Ehle (1873–1949) confirmed Johannsen's ideas examining color inheritance in wheat grains. Red always was dominant to white, but varied in intensity. By crossing reds with whites he found the offspring fell into three distinct groups, but each group exhibited a range of variation around a mean. He explained his results by postulating that three different genes contributed to the red color and that they segregated independently of one another. By crossing the homozygous white with a red, having only one red gene would be enough to turn the grain red, but how intense it would be would depend on the number of red alleles that were inherited. Effects of the environment would also influence the growth and color and yield offspring that showed a range of variation. The effects of the environment would further smooth out the differences yielding a continuous variation just like Johannsen had observed in his pure lines.

Both men's work showed that only the variation due to the genotype, rather than the environment, was inherited and this was further evidence against Lamarckian inheritance. It also showed that the individual mutation could be much smaller than de Vries envisioned; and due to multigene inheritance the continuous range of variation observed in the wild could be explained by the principles of Mendelian inheritance. Nevertheless, Johannsen thought that natural selection acting on continuous variation could not shift the genotypes. It could only prefer one to another within the population. He thought that mutation still was what was responsible for creating something new for selection to act on. The mutations might be small, but they were what drove evolution. Thomas Morgan's (1866–1945) breeding experiments with the fruit fly *Drosophila melanogaster* provided evidence for such a position. In one of his pure lines a single white-eyed male appeared which he then crossed with the normal red-eyed females. The first cross resulted in all red-eyed offspring, and the next generation produced a 3:1 ratio of red to white-eyed offspring, demonstrating that the white allele character was recessive. Morgan deliberately used the word mutation to describe this sudden change in the gene for red eye, producing a new allele for white. Morgan's lab became known as the fly room of Columbia University where hundreds of thousands of flies were bred. What was found was virtually a continual stream of new mutations spontaneously appearing which were then used not only to unravel the mechanism of heredity, but also eventually to reconcile the ideas of the Mendelians and the Darwinians.

Building on the work of biometricians and the breeding experiments of Nilsson-Ehle, William Castle (1867–1962), and others, a new group of geneticists pioneered a mathematical approach that combined biometrics and Mendelian genetics, and looked at effects of selection and systems of mating to build quantitative models of the evolutionary process. G. H. Hardy (1877–1947) in 1908 showed what the distribution of a pair of alleles "A" and "a" would be in a population with no selection. The possible genotypes were aa, AA or Aa. If the alleles were present initially in a ratio of $A = p$ and $a = q$ then $p + q = 1$. Using Mendel's laws of inheritance, and assuming independent mating, the frequency of the alleles in the next generation can be determined by the equation $p^2 + 2pq + q^2 = 1$. Furthermore, the proportion of the two alleles A and a would remain constant in future generations if nothing upset this equilibrium. This became known as the **Hardy–Weinberg equilibrium** because Wilhelm Weinberg independently discovered the same principle. This was a highly simplified model of what happened in nature. Selection, non-random mating, and migration in and out of the population were all factors that would disturb this equilibrium. The mathematician H. T. J. Norton was one of the first to recognize the significance of Hardy's work and showed that even a slight advantage of 10 percent or less could change the frequency of a gene in a population. He based this on data on mimicry in butterflies. Selection was powerful.

Ronald Fisher (1892–1962) continued to build on these ideas modeling the effects of variation, drift, mutation, and selection on gene frequency and demonstrated that evolution occurred gradually by selection acting on small genetic differences. His book *Genetical Theory of Natural Selection* (1930) summarized the key ideas that had emerged. First, there was no inherent tendency for variability to diminish over time. As Mendel and Hardy had shown, genes were for the most part maintained through successive generations. Second, genes lost through drift or by chance had significant effects only in small isolated populations. Third, although populations contained high levels of variability, new mutations were relatively rare. Since organisms were already reasonably well adapted, these new forms tended to be deleterious and they would be quickly weeded out by selection. Forth and most important, Fisher had shown by his calculations that selection was by far the most important factor in changing the gene frequencies of a population. He also showed that selection created what was known as balanced **polymorphism** where two or more distinct forms of a species inhabit the same area. One allele might have a selective advantage up to a certain frequency, but then become disadvantageous above it. If the heterozygote had a selective advantage over both homozygotes then a stable equilibrium between the two alleles would be maintained. This contributed to maintaining high levels of variation. J. B. S. Haldane (1892–1964), another mathematical biologist, came to the same conclusions and applied his calculations to a real case: industrial melanism of the peppered moth. The peppered moth was light-colored to blend in with the lichen that covered most of the light-colored trees. As a result of the Industrial Revolution pollution killed most of the lichen and the trees became covered with soot. In 1848 the first black form of the moth was recorded near Manchester, England. By 1895 it had almost totally replaced the normal peppered grey one found in that area. The black form was due to a single **dominant gene** and Haldane worked out that for it to have spread through the population that quickly it must have had a selective advantage of about 30 percent. This was an indication that selection intensities might be much stronger in nature than Fisher had suggested. Castle provided additional evidence of the power of selection and the importance of gene interactions in his breeding experiments with different colored hooded rats. The black- and white-hooded pattern appeared to be inherited as a simple recessive to the dominant grey. Yet the pattern was quite variable and by selective breeding Castle was able to establish strains that were practically all white or all black that were quite stable. To return them to the original pattern was just as difficult as the original selection. Nevertheless, back crossing the strains with homozygous grey rats resulted in offspring with highly variable amounts of black and white in their coat color. This showed that a trait was not determined just by a single gene, but instead could be modified by interaction with other genes. This also meant that a single gene probably also influenced a variety of different traits. Multiple effects of single genes had been well documented in *Drosophila* and was called **pleiotropy**, which resulted in each offspring being a little different than the parents. This suggested that there was an enormous store of variation "hidden" in the genome available for natural selection to act on. As Castle wrote, this meant that natural selection was an agency of real creative power.

Castle's student Sewall Wright (1889–1988) continued Castle's breeding experiments with rats and also did his own on the inheritance of coat color in guinea pigs, which he continued long after he left Castle's lab. He developed new methods to analyze the results and came to the conclusion that selection was most effective on groups of interacting genes. As a result of constant inbreeding he found that the families became more and more different from each other, but also more and more homozygous. It appeared that certain genes became lost while others became fixed, but it was a matter of chance as to what combinations became fixed in particular families. This random fluctuation resulting in changes in relative gene frequency is called **genetic drift**. Wright applied this thinking to evolution in the wild and argued that selection would be most effective in small populations, which by chance might have frequencies of certain genes that were not representative of the species as a whole. This in turn would lead to combinations that became fixed, unlikely to occur in a larger population because of gene flow among individuals. Selection would be able to act on these combinations in the small populations more efficiently and the species would evolve more quickly. This became known as Wright's "shifting balance theory of evolution." That genetic drift and selection in small populations played a more significant role than selection acting on single genes in large populations caused quite a dispute between Wright and Fisher and Haldane. Wright himself changed his mind about the importance of drift and by the 1960s relegated it to a relatively minor role in evolution. In spite of the differences between Wright and the other two, all of them agreed that mutation by itself was relatively powerless to cause a significant change in gene frequencies. This contradicted the views of Bateson and de Vries. Furthermore, what had appeared to be two different kinds of variation, the continuous variation found in nature and the discontinuous variation observed in artificial selection, were shown to follow the same rules of Mendelian inheritance. The continuous variation observed in nature was the product not only of the action of environment, but also due to the fact that many genes influenced the same trait. Due to multiple-gene inheritance it was possible to produce populations that exhibited variation that went beyond the limits of that observed in the parent populations. Population genetics modeling had demonstrated unequivocally that over time new species would result from selection acting gradually on discrete and usually quite small mutations. This was a critical finding since one of the most consistent criticisms of Darwin's theory from Huxley to de Vries had been that natural selection did not have the power to actually create new species.

THE MODERN SYNTHESIS

The 1940s gave rise to what Julian Huxley (1887–1975) (grandson of Thomas) dubbed the Modern Synthesis in his book *Evolution: The Modern Synthesis* (1942). Several books that are still considered classics all built on and provided additional evidence from a variety of disciplines in support of Darwin's theory. Ernst Mayr (1904–2005) emphasized the role of geographic factors in speciation in *Systematics and the Origin of the Species* (1942). Based on his extensive fieldwork on birds in the Solomon Islands and New Guinea as well as other research, he argued that new species usually arose from races or subspecies that had become geographically isolated. Just as Darwin had claimed, these could be regarded as incipient species. If traits evolved that reduced or prevented interbreeding among the parent populations during the period of isolation, then even if the geographical barrier was removed later, enough differences had accumulated that one species had become two. He called this **allopatric speciation**, contrasting it with sympatric speciation in which new species arise even in the absence of any geographical barrier. With many more fossils available than in Darwin's time, paleontologists also provided support to Darwin's idea of slow gradual change. In *Tempo and Mode in Evolution* G. G. Simpson (1902–84) claimed that **macroevolution** (evolution at or above the level of species, over geologic time resulting in the formation of new taxonomic groups) as revealed by the fossil record could be explained by the accumulated effects of microevolutionary processes occurring at the population level. For example, the fossil record of the horse revealed a pattern of gradual branching evolution. Rather than a straight linear line as others had argued, at each stage four or five different lineages arose each with its own distinct set of toes and teeth. In *Variation and Evolution in Plants* (1950) George Ledyard Stebbins Jr (1906– 2000) elucidated the genetic mechanisms of plant evolution. **Polyploidy** (having more than the usual **diploid** number of chromosomes) along with hybridization was relatively common in the plant world compared to the animal kingdom, and Stebbins showed that it played a significant role in the development of complex and widespread genera, but also that it was common in relatively few families. Thus these processes had not played a major role in overall plant evolution.

Consistently cited by both working scientists and historians as the pivotal work of the synthesis period, was Theodosius Dobzhansky's (1900–975) *Evolution and the Origin of the Species* (1937). A geneticist who had emigrated from Russia and started working in Morgan's fly lab, Dobzhansky brought with him a populational approach that looked at the genetics of natural populations. Dobzhansky's work was critical to bridging the gap between what the field naturalists were observing in the wild and the abstract mathematical modeling of population geneticists. He summarized the experimental evidence that illuminated the true nature of mutations, showing that their effects might be small but at the same time contributed to the enormous variability that existed in natural populations. An example that remains highly relevant today is, he showed, how selection could account for the rise of strains of scale insects that were resistant to cyanide gas. The gas had been used to control them in the citrus groves of California. Looking at how species form, his research confirmed what Mayr was also finding. Dobzhansky argued that species or even races differ from one another by many genes making it virtually impossible for a new species to arise by one single step or mutation. It would take time for the different gene combinations to accumulate, and interbreeding would continually break up such combinations. Thus some kind of isolating mechanism must take place, geographical being the most obvious. However, geographical isolation often was only temporary. To preserve separate populations other kinds of isolating mechanisms would need to come into play, and careful field observations confirmed this was exactly what had happened. Occupying different habitats, even within the same area, or mating at different times of the year were all mechanisms for maintaining isolation. Changes in courtship behavior or the reproductive organs might also prevent copulation. The subspecies or populations would continue to diverge and become so different that geographical isolation was no longer needed. A species was not an arbitrary unit of classification, but represented a distinct biological entity that was reproductively isolated from other species. That being said, however, what was ranked as a species as opposed to a subspecies or race was often not clear-cut in species that had wide ranges. For example, may species of birds have distinct populations, their members capable of breeding with members of the neighboring populations. Yet two birds from each end of the range could not interbreed and behaved as good biological species. This research demonstrated the importance of local populations for evolution, and provided clear evidence for gradual evolution. From 1938 onward, Dobzhansky collaborated with Wright and demonstrated that selection was not just a mechanism of change, but could also act to maintain stability through a variety of mechanisms such as superior heterozygote fitness. An important example of heterozygote fitness in humans is the maintenance of the sickle cell gene in areas where malaria is pre-valent. The sickle cell gene causes a defective form of hemoglobin that causes red blood cells to collapse when deprived of oxygen, resulting in misshapen cells. They can get stuck in vessels, causing dangerous clots, and are also destroyed by white blood cells that recognize them as defective. Having two copies of this gene causes anemia and even death. The parasite that causes malaria lives in the red blood cells, however. Thus the destruction of these abnormal red blood cells also destroys the parasite. Having only one copy of the gene then often allows a person to survive a bout of malaria and yet at the same time, since the person also has one normal copy, this prevents severe anemia.

The synthesis period was an era of collaborative research that brought the ideas of naturalists and population geneticists together. It vindicated Darwin's claim that evolution occurred by the gradual accumulation of small inherited variations, and that the primary mechanism of change was natural selection. Mendelism triumphed and Lamarckian forms of inheritance along with the mutation theory were thoroughly discredited. However, as historian Will Provine pointed out, it might be more appropriate to refer to this period as the evolutionary constriction. Dobzhanksy's redefining evolution as changes in gene frequency resulted in population genetics exerting a virtual monopoly as the only discipline that could significantly contribute to advancing the theoretical aspects of Darwin's theory. Disciplines such as paleontology and field research were labeled as merely descriptive, and relegated to the role of providing confirmation of the abstract formulations of the ever more sophisticated modeling of the geneticists. Yet this modeling had really only demonstrated the transformation of populations and not the origin of new taxa. Although Darwin considered embryology the most important evidence in favor of his theory, it was essentially left out of the synthesis. Stephen Gould (1941–2002) referred to the period of the 1950s as the "hardening of the synthesis." Evolution, however, proved ever resilient. Gould and Niles Eldredge led the way in demonstrating the importance of paleontology to the theory of evolution with their theory of punctuated equili-brium in the 1970s and 1980s and also suggested the importance of embryology as well. Today integrating development with evolution is considered absolutely critical for evolution to maintain its status as the great unifying idea of biology. Advances in genetics, most importantly the discovery of DNA as the hereditary material and the elucidation of its structure, ushered in several new areas of research, creating new areas of controversy, but at the same time continuing to provide evidence at the deepest levels of biology in support of evolution.

FURTHER READING

Dobzanksy, T. (1937) *Genetics and the Origin of Species,* New York: Columbia University Press.

Mayr, E., Provine, W. (eds) (1998) *The Evolutionary Synthesis: Perspectives on the Unification of Biology*, Cambridge, MA: Harvard University Press.

Provine, W. (1971) *The Origins of Theoretical Population Genetics,* Chicago: University of Chicago Press.

——(1986) *Sewall Wright: Geneticist and Evolutionist,* Chicago: University of Chicago Press.

4

EXPANDING THE MODERN SYNTHESIS

DNA: EVOLUTION AT THE MOLECULAR LEVEL

The elucidation of the structure of DNA (deoxyribonucleic acid) by James Watson and Francis Crick in 1953 began what often has been referred to as a revolution in biology. For a long time protein was thought to be the carrier of hereditary material. In the words of many biochemists, nucleic acid was a "stupid molecule," i.e. it couldn't possibly have the specificity or variety to encode information. The hereditary material must do three things. It must (1) have a way of duplicating itself, (2) have a way of encoding information, and (3) be able to exert a highly specific influence on the cell. In the 1950s and 1960s scientists worked out in exquisite detail how DNA carried out all of these functions. The structure was confirmed, the details of DNA replication were explained, and the discovery of several different classes of RNA (ribonucleic acid) and the subsequent "breaking of the hereditary code" enabled scientists to show how DNA's third function was carried out. This ultimately led to the human genome project and has ushered in a whole new era of molecular medicine with the potential for gene therapy and genetic engineering of organisms. It provided evidence for evolution at the deepest level, allowing us to investigate evolutionary processes at the molecular level. Potentially we now have the means to alter the course of evolution, which has profound ethical implications.

DNA is a long double-chained molecule with the two chains twisting around one another forming a double helix. Each chain consists of the sugar deoxyribose alternating with phosphate as its backbone. Attached to the sugar is one of four bases: adenine (A), guanine (G), cytosine (C), or thymine (T). The bases can be attached in any order along one chain and the two chains are held together by hydrogen bonding between the bases. However, the base pairing is very specific. A can only pair with T and G only pairs with C. Thus A always = T and G = C, but the ratio of AT to GC can and does vary from organism to organism. This structure immediately suggested how DNA might carry out its first two functions. The long sequence of bases can be in any order, making possible a virtually infinite number of permutations. The specific sequence of the bases is the actual carrier of genetic information, providing the instructions for making proteins, which include enzymes that drive virtually all the chemical processes that occur inside the cell. The specific base pairing means that each chain is complementary to the other. During replication the two chains break apart, each serving as a template to make a new molecule. Two new molecules result, each made up of one old chain and one newly synthesized one. DNA is sequestered in the nucleus, but exerts its influence on the cell by another closely related molecule, messenger ribonucleic acid (mRNA), in a series of processes called **transcription** and **translation**. See **Figure 4.1**. RNA is similar to DNA, but also different. It is single stranded, and instead of deoxyribose, the sugar is ribose, and uracil replaces thymine. The genetic code actually refers to the sequence of bases in the mRNA molecule rather than DNA although the RNA sequence is determined by the corresponding sequence in the DNA molecule. The code is a triplet code, meaning that three bases called a **codon** specify a particular amino acid along with specific codons that mean "start" or "stop." A particular section of the DNA is transcribed by mRNA binding to it by means of complementary base pairing with U substituting for T. The mRNA then leaves the nucleus where it is translated with the help of two other types of RNA, ribosomal (rRNA) and transfer (tRNA), to make a protein molecule. There are several aspects to this process that are significant for evolution. First, the code is highly redundant. Four bases in combinations of three means there are 64 different codons, but for the most part only 20 different amino acids are used in cell metabolism. Therefore several codons code for the same amino acid. Usually, changing the

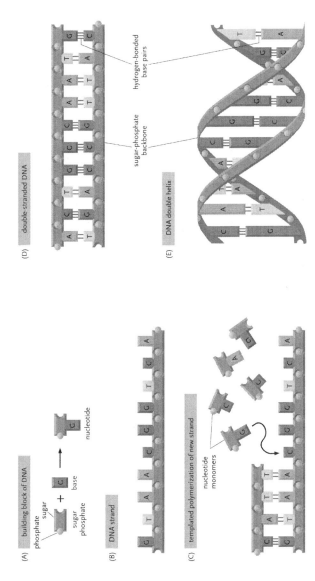

(A) building block of DNA

phosphate
sugar

base

sugar
phosphate

nucleotide

(B) DNA strand

(C) templated polymerization of new strand

nucleotide
monomers

(D) double-stranded DNA

hydrogen-bonded
base pairs

(E) DNA double helix

sugar-phosphate
backbone

Figure 4.1 DNA and its building blocks. DNA, the hereditary molecule, is a very long molecule built of units, called nucleotides, that consist of a nitrogenous base, a phosphate group, and deoxyribose sugar

Source: *Molecular Biology of the Cell*, 5th edition, Figures 1–2, p. 3

third base of each codon results in the same amino acid being coded for. This is a safeguard because it allows for a certain amount of inaccuracy in copying and will not create any problems. In this regard an error in base pairing is much less serious than either an addition or deletion of a base, because when the latter occurs, the whole reading frame is shifted. Instead of one amino acid being off, potentially every one would be changed (see **Figure 4.2**). Second, hydrogen bonding is very specific, but also a relatively weak bond. Not only does that mean it can be broken easily for copying or transcribing, but this also means that base pairing errors will occur. We don't want too many, but errors are the raw material for natural selection to act on. Once the structure of DNA was known

The Genetic Code				
1st position (5 end)	2nd Position			3rd Position (3 end)
U	U	C	A	G
U	Phe	Ser	Tyr	Cys	U
	Phe	Ser	Tyr	Cys	C
	Leu	Ser	STOP	STOP	A
	Leu	Ser	STOP	Trp	G
C	Leu	Pro	His	Arg	U
	Leu	Pro	His	Arg	C
	Leu	Pro	Gln	Arg	A
	Leu	Pro	Gln	Arg	G
A	Ile	Thr	Asn	Ser	U
	Ile	Thr	Asn	Ser	C
	Ile	Thr	Lys	Arg	A
	Met	Thr	Lys	Arg	G
G	Val	Ala	Asp	Gly	U
	Val	Ala	Asp	Gly	C
	Val	Ala	Glu	Gly	A
	Val	Ala	Glu	Gly	G

Figure 4.2 The genetic code. The same mRNA codons specify the same amino acids in all life on Earth. The genetic code is therefore universal – there is no "human genetic code"

Source: Adapted from *Molecular Biology of the Cell*, 5th edition, Figure T:1

mutations could be defined precisely. They are changes in the sequence of bases in the DNA and are what create variability. Sometimes just a single change can make a profound difference. In sickle cell anemia, only one amino acid substitution has occurred, as the result of one base substitution, but this was enough to create a defective hemoglobin molecule that causes the red cell to have a sickle shape. Yet in environments where malaria is prevalent, having one copy of this gene is beneficial because the sickle cell is a less favorable environment for the parasite to live in. This was one of our earliest examples of documenting natural selection at the molecular level. Many variants of the hemoglobin molecule have been found and they may be beneficial in particular environments. Third, as was pointed out in **Chapter 1**, the genetic code is universal. Many different bacteria and other organisms such as yeast (important for the brewing industry) have been converted into molecular factories to make all kinds of molecules from virtually any species. They can "read" the instructions correctly because all species use the same universal language. The universality of the genetic code is powerful evidence that all life has descended from one or a few common ancestors.

As researchers started to sequence more and more DNA, they made a surprising discovery. The amount of genetic variability was enormous, far more than what was observed at the level of the phenotype. Sequencing also led to the discovery of introns (short for intervening sequences) and exons (sequences that code for amino acids), Making up an enormous percentage of DNA, the introns appeared not to code for anything and were referred to as junk DNA. It was transcribed, but then cut out. Only the exon sequences were translated. The term junk has persisted, but it is not really appropriate. It is now known that some introns do encode information for RNAs that control gene expression and some are actually exons on the complementary strand of the DNA. While some introns may be vestiges of ancient genes that have lost their original function and are "junk," still this exon/intron organization provides another mechanism for generating diversity. Diversity is the key to evolutionary success. Different combinations of exons of the same gene result in different versions of the same protein product. This is a possible explanation of how cell types use a particular protein in slightly different ways in different tissues as well as make available variants for natural selection to act on.

MOOTO KIMURA AND THE NEUTRAL THEORY OF SELECTION

The sequence data indicated that at the level of the DNA most base substitutions were selectively neutral, and provided evidence in support of Motoo Kimura's (1924–94) **neutral theory** of evolution. In 1968 he argued that most of the changes at the level of DNA were not the result of natural selection selecting for advantageous mutations, but instead were the result of the random fixation of selectively neutral mutants. This was in a sense an extension of Wright's theory of genetic drift, verified at the molecular level. The neutral theory claimed that only a tiny fraction of variability observed at the molecular level was adaptive. The protein and DNA polymorphisms represented a transient phase of molecular evolution that was maintained by a balance between mutational input and random extinction, rather than by some form of balancing selection. One of the predictions from the neutral theory is that non-coding DNA would evolve much faster than the coding regions. This is exactly what has been found. Such DNA sequences accumulate far more base substitutions because they do not matter, confirming the neutral theory. However, controversy remains over changes in the functional regions of the DNA. Whether the enormous variability observed at the level of protein is essentially neutral rather than adaptive remains an open question and has led to the burgeoning of **proteomics**, i.e. the sequencing of proteins. Whether many of the slight variants of a particular protein have any functional significance is being decided on a case-by-case basis. Many people argue that natural selection will eliminate base substitutions that result in a defective final product. Thus natural selection would still be the primary force in determining the course of adaptive evolution, and the neutral theory does not represent any significant challenge to this idea.

A MOLECULAR CLOCK FOR DETERMINING ANCESTRY

Regardless of the eventual status of the neutral theory, Kimura's work on how random processes had differing effects on mutation, depending on whether the mutation was neutral, beneficial, or deleterious, had important ramifications. It led to the idea of a **molecular clock**, which made it possible to compare genes between different species, and see how similar they were to develop a molecular phylogeny, i.e. the evolutionary development and history of a species or higher taxonomic grouping of organisms. Sequence data showed that for those regions of DNA that code for protein, the rate that one neutral base substituted for another was simply the mutation rate and was remarkably constant. Since mutation rates were reasonably well known, it was possible to date more accurately when branching and divergence occurred by examining sequence data of **homologous** genes. The mutations can be regarded as the ticks of a molecular clock. By counting the number of ticks or accumulated mutations in the same region of the DNA in different species, and plotting it against the branch points that were well known from the fossil record, it was possible to determine when different species diverged from a common ancestor. However, different genes evolve at different rates and thus the most effective ones to determine phylogeny are those that are highly conserved, for example those that have to do with basic energy metabolism such as cytochrome-c. The 104 amino acid sequence of cytochrome-c is identical in humans and chimpanzees. The human sequence differs by 1 amino acid from rhesus monkeys, by 11 additional ones from horses and an additional 21 from tuna.

Molecular sequence data is not without its problems. Each gene represents a different clock, ticking away at a different rate. Thus depending on which gene one picks, different phylogenies can be constructed. Furthermore, the amount of variation observed is even more than would be predicted by a constant mutation rate, i.e. each "clock" may have periods when it has speeded up or slowed down and this has resulted in differing evolutionary rates among differing lineages. Nevertheless, molecular data has some distinct advantages over other methods of determining ancestry as well as timing of divergence. First, the information is far more quantifiable than examining traits by traditional methods of comparative anatomy and embryology. For example, sequence data has shown unequivocally that dogs have descended only from wolves, with no input from coyotes. It also shows that domestication of wolves may have occurred more than once. Second, it provides a way of comparing organisms that have relatively little **morphology** to build a phylogeny such as bacteria and other single-celled organisms. Furthermore, it has made possible comparisons between widely differing organisms. It is difficult to compare an amoeba, an orchid, a cat and a human, based on morphology. However, DNA and protein sequence analysis has provided some astonishing information. Not only is our DNA extremely similar to that of a chimp (current estimates range between 95 and 99 percent depending on how the comparison is being made), but we also share a large number of genes with fruit flies and yeast. Although we associate evolution with the idea of change, sequence data has revealed that evolution is basically a conservative process with gene sequences being maintained for millions of years across widely different taxa. The platypus has always been a conundrum, looking like it has been stitched together from widely different organisms having characteristics of birds (webbed feet and the bill of a duck), reptiles (rubbery eggs and venomous spines) and mammals (fur and feeds its young with milk, although it doesn't have nipples). Sequence data has confirmed exactly that. It had been classified as a monotreme, a group of mammals that shared its last common ancestor with the group that gave rise to humans between 160 and 200 million years ago (mya). It is a mammal, but has maintained traits that are considered primitive, meaning that it has retained traits from early mammalian ancestors such as egg laying that have been lost in the lineages that gave rise to cats and us. Often, based on traditional methods it is difficult to determine what is a primitive and what is a derived trait in order to build an accurate family tree. However, as more and more organisms have their genes sequenced, it will be possible to examine as many genes as necessary to resolve conflicting data regarding the building of phylogenies. As we will see in **Chapter 6**, it has revolutionized our thinking about the classification of simple organisms and allowed us to extend our investigation to the early forms of life by another billion years.

NATURAL SELECTION IN ACTION

Darwin's finches have continued to have iconic significance for the theory of evolution. The ornithologist David Lack (1910–73) visited the Galapagos in 1938–39, and initially thought that selection on the finches was weak on the islands, due to the absence of predators and competitors for food. He thought that the differences in beaks were primarily a result of genetic drift, but he changed his mind as a result of reconsidering his detailed observations. He saw the beaks were designed to exploit different food sources, such as small seeds, large seeds, nuts, insects, and fruits. Natural selection had produced highly specialized and adapted forms that minimized competition. Lack focused on cases where several species existed in the same location, occupying the same ecology. Competition would be especially intense and he thought this would result in one species totally eliminating the others. This is exactly what had happened. On small islands only one species of ground finch existed. On the larger islands where more than one species existed, he found they differentiated themselves by occupying different environmental niches, such as feeding on different kinds of food or living in slightly different habitats. One species might be found primarily on the ground while another was found in the treetops. Lack's work was particularly important at the time because it documented natural selection in the wild as opposed to much of the work being done by the population geneticists analyzing cases of artificial selection. Lack's work was extended and confirmed by the long-term studies of finches done by Rosemary and Peter Grant.

Beginning in 1973, the Grants and their team spent six months of every year on Daphne Major and through painstakingly detailed measurements documented that evolution was not something that took thousands of years to see. It was happening right before their very eyes. They measured the size and shape of the beaks, the quantity and types of seeds eaten and various other traits of two different species of finches as the climate cycled through wet and dry seasons. Who survived and who didn't? In 1977 the rain never came and the severe drought resulted in a shortage of food and the small soft seeds favored by the birds quickly disappeared. Birds who had bigger strong beaks that could open the tough bigger seeds differentially survived and shifted the population in the direction of larger beaks. In 1984–85 an unusually wet season produced an abundance of small seeds and favored those birds with smaller beaks. Significant change in beak size occurred within just a few generations. Furthermore, the two species have begun to hybridize more frequently. Although no new species has yet emerged, a particular trend, such as a long period of extended drought, would undoubtedly push certain species to extinction while other ones would emerge.

DNA analysis has confirmed exactly what Darwin originally hypothesized. The 14 species of finches share a common ancestor.

They are more similar to each other than to grassquit, the most closely related bird on the mainland. Darwin's finches evolved from a grassquit-like ancestral population that arrived from the mainland a few million years ago and eventually gave rise to four different lineages of finches. The warbler finches have a slender beak to catch insects while the finches in the vegetarian lineage have stubby beaks to eat buds, fruit and flower blossoms. Later two more groups emerged, the ground finches with beaks adapted to eat seeds and the tree finches that catch insects in trees. This includes the woodpecker finch that uses a cactus spine in its beak to dig out insects in the cracks of trees. Although ornithologists have classified the ground finches into six different species, according to DNA analysis they are really species in the making, barely formed. Their DNA is distinct from the other lineages, but among themselves, they are still mating with one another successfully. In addition, finches from other islands occasionally come to Daphne. All of this is helping maintain enormous stores of variability that will enable the finches to continue to evolve in response to continually changing environmental conditions.

An even more dramatic example of rapid adaptive radiation has occurred in Lake Victoria in Africa. Five hundred species of cichlid fish exist and are endemic to this lake (meaning found nowhere else). Several factors have contributed to the enormous number of cichlid species. The lake is a very stable environment that encourages speciation. In a rapidly changing environment, it pays to be a generalist, to be able to adapt to the changing conditions and to maintain one large interbreeding population that keeps high levels of variability within it. Being highly adapted to a particular environment in the short term is highly advantageous, but if the environment keeps changing then it is a ticket to extinction. However, being stable is not the same as being homogenous and Lake Victoria has many different micro-environments, including rocky shores, smooth sandy bottoms, deep and shallow water. This has allowed these brightly colored fish to specialize in many different ways that minimize competition. Changes in the upper jaw have resulted in teeth becoming different kinds of tools: spikes, pegs or spatulas each adapted for a different kind of food supply whether it be crushing shell fish or scraping off algae from rocks. The lower jaw is used for breaking up and digesting vegetable matter. The cichlid common ancestor was a mouthbrooder (carrying the eggs in its mouth), which meant that males no longer had to guard the eggs and sexual selection became an enormous factor in generating diversity. Difference in color, the shape of fins as well as elaborate and differing courtship rituals all evolved, contributing to rapid speciation. Cichlids are also secondary freshwater fish, meaning that they evolved from saltwater fish and have a high tolerance for salt. This allows them to exploit different micro-environments, such as along the rocky shores, that have higher levels of dissolved minerals and saltier water. In 1995 geologists made an astonishing discovery. Examining the strata they found that the lake totally dried up between 14,000 and 12,000 years ago. This meant that all the species that exist in the lake today could not have originated any earlier than 14,000 years ago. DNA analysis confirmed this recent origin and showed that the cichlids were all descended from one lineage found in the rivers and streams of east Africa, which in turn was derived from one single lineage of maternal mouthbrooder cichlids from Lake Tanganyika. They are only distantly related to cichlids from other lakes or rivers.

Sadly, the cichlids are another cautionary tale of the impact that humans are having on diversity. In Darwin's time several species of Galapagos tortoises had already been eaten into extinction. Countless numbers of species have gone extinct as a result of humans altering and destroying their habitat. Lake Victoria is a microcosm of what is happening all over the world. In the 1950s the Nile perch was introduced into Lake Victoria as a source of food for humans. It thrived, growing quite large on its diet of cichlids. Farming and logging caused massive erosion, dumping enormous amounts of topsoil into the lake and turning the once clear water murky. The cichlids can no longer see the characteristic markings of their particular species and are often mating with closely related species, breaking down the reproductive isolation that existed. In a mere 30 years over half of the cichlid species have disappeared due to the Nile perch and the cloudy water.

MACROEVOLUTION: THE PACE AND PATTERN OF EVOLUTIONARY CHANGE

Darwin was committed to the idea that the process of evolution was slow and gradual. However, as Huxley had pointed out, the fossil record exhibited a pattern of species abruptly appearing and disappearing with very few transitional organisms. Although Huxley eventually gave up his saltational views, the issue of saltation resurfaced in various different guises throughout the twentieth century. De Vries' mutation theory claimed that species-level change only occurred by natural selection acting on large mutations. Although gradualism became firmly embedded in evolutionary theory primarily due to the work of population geneticists in the 1920s, culminating in the Modern Synthesis of the 1940s and 1950s, it always had its critics. Geneticist Richard Goldschmidt (1878–1958) and paleontologist O. H. Schindewolf (1896–1971) both believed macroevolution could not be explained by microevolutionary mechanisms. Goldschmidt claimed that the accumulation of little mutations could only lead to diversification within a species to adapt to local conditions, but that evolutionarily they were essentially blind alleys and were not a model for the origin of new species. He argued that some other kind of mechanism was necessary such as a systemic mutant that essentially created a new species in one large step, a "hopeful monster." In what was regarded as a highly heretical statement he claimed that the "first bird hatched from a dinosaur's egg." This has turned out not to be so heretical since as is discussed below, he was essentially correct, but not for the reasons he thought. However, Goldschmidt was roundly criticized and discredited, particularly by Mayr who claimed that his work on geographic factors in the role of speciation was in part stimulated by his opposition to Goldschmidt's ideas. Simpson was highly critical of Schindewolf whose macroevolutionary theory was embedded in a grandiose cosmic theory of everything that hearkened back to the nineteenth-century *Naturphilosophen*. Nevertheless, in *Tempo and Mode* Simpson devoted a section to what he called quantum evolution and suggested that something other than microevolutionary processes was at play in evolution above the species level. He pointed out that in spite of millions of fossils being found, gaps remained, particularly in regard to new "types," i.e. the origin of higher taxa. He suggested that paleontology had unique advantages for studying evolution. Population genetics "may reveal what happens to a hundred rats in the course of 10 years, under fixed and simple conditions, but not what happened to a billion rats in the course of a million years under the fluctuating conditions of earth history." However, in *The Major Features of Evolution* (1953), essentially a revised and updated version of *Tempo and Mode*, Simpson left out his section on quantum evolution. The synthesis had indeed "hardened." Saltational evolution received its most serious hearing with the theory of punctuated equilibrium.

PUNCTUATED EQUILIBRIUM

In 1972 Niles Eldredge and Stephen Gould challenged the Darwinian paradigm of slow, gradual change, which they called **phyletic gradualism** with their theory of punctuated equilibria. They argued that the fossil record documented a pattern of periods of rapid diversification interspersed with periods of relatively little change or stasis. Since Darwin's time sampling of the fossil record had become far more extensive and carefully done. Radiometric dating made possible the dating of fossils more accurately and now molecular sequence data is extending our reach into the past even further. Yet explaining the pattern of the fossil record has remained problematic. Indeed, Gould and Eldredge began their 1977 paper on punctuated equilibrium with Huxley's caution to Darwin about burdening his theory unnecessarily with the idea that nature doesn't make jumps. The details of the debate have changed, but the underlying issues remain the same. First is the question of gaps. In spite of millions more fossils being found, systematic gaps remain. Gould and Eldredge argued that the gaps were not due to an incomplete record, but rather were real and reflected how evolution was occurring. However, we continue to find transitional organisms. The following are just a few examples. A turtle dating from about 200 mya was found in China. However, it had a shell only on its belly, had teeth and a long pointed snout, in contrast to modern turtles with their complete body covering, short snout and no teeth. A toothed amphibian dated at about 290 mya was recently discovered. Its combination of features such as a wide skull and the structure of its ear drum (like a frog) and fused ankle bones (like a salamander) suggest it may have been close to the origins of both modern frogs and salamanders. *Basilosaurus* is a whale-like creature with feet, and from Eocene rocks in Pakistan we have accumulated a very good record of the transition in body form from a four-legged terrestrial ungulate to a fish-shaped whale that documents the return of mammals to the sea. The discovery of Tiktaalik, a lobe-finned fish that lived about 375 mya has many features similar to those of tetrapods and represents a transitional organism between fish and land-based animals. They show the beginning of adaptations that will eventually allow their descendants such as amphibians to emerge from the sea. Ever since Huxley first suggested that dinosaurs were the connecting links between birds and reptiles we have continued to find fossils of birds that were more and more dinosaur-like and dinosaurs that were more and more bird-like, culminating with the discovery in the 1990s of the feathered dinosaurs. Birds are dinosaurs and most paleontologists think that they evolved from theropods, although some alternative phylogenies have been suggested. However, the main point is that transitional organisms continue to be found that unite more and more widely separated groups as well as filling in the gaps in particular lineages.

Related to but distinct from the question of the gaps is the rate of evolution. Although Darwin acknowledged that different lineages had variable evolutionary rates, he thought they were all changing more or less continuously. This is referred to as **anagenesis**. After enough time a lineage may have changed so much that it has become a new species known as a **chronospecies**. Sometimes new species were created by splitting, known as **cladogenesis**, but the rate was no faster or slower than the normal rates of lineage evolution. Speciation was thus primarily a by-product of anagenesis. Punctuated equilibrium claimed that the rate of evolution was jerky. Instead of one species gradually changing into another, speciation was rapid with most morphological change occurring at the time of branching speciation. Cladogenesis rather than anagenesis was the more important process in creating change. Eldredge and Gould maintained this represented a more accurate view of how the fossil record actually looked. See **Figure 4.3**. Most fossil species stayed the same through many meters of sediment representing hundreds of thousands if not millions of years (stasis) and then looked quite different or disappeared. Eldredge and Gould basically took Mayr's idea of allopatric or geographic speciation and applied it temporally, to the geological record. If this was the main mechanism of speciation one would not even expect to find in the fossil record a pattern of gradual divergence of two populations that had become geographically isolated.

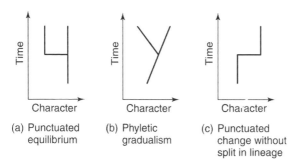

Figure 4.3 Phyletic gradualism contrasted with punctuated equilibrium

Punctuated equilibrium was hotly debated throughout the 1970s and 1980s, but even its harshest critics admitted that it stimulated and revitalized debate among evolutionary biologists, particularly paleontologists. Today, it is acknowledged that the fossil record exhibits both kinds of patterns. Although punctuated equilibrium was a theory about the pattern in the fossil record and rates of change, not about mechanism, it meant that the question of macroevolution was revisited. Several important ideas emerged. First, stasis was data. It was important to explain not just why/how organisms change, but also why they do not. The pattern of stasis was too widespread to be ignored. Russell Lande developed quantitative genetic models that explained such a pattern and claimed the pattern did not represent any significant challenge to the neo-Darwinian paradigm. Second was the notion of hierarchy. The cause and explanation of how adaptation occurs in local populations and speciation were often different, i.e. selection acts at different levels. It can act at the level of the gene, at the level of the organism, and also at the level of species. Steven Stanley argued that the species was a legitimate agent of evolutionary change and that it was a mistake to conflate genetics with evolution. Dobzanksy's often quoted definition that evolution is a change in gene frequencies tells us nothing about the pattern and process that led to that change. Like Gould and Eldredge, Stanley maintained that most of the important changes that were observable in the record appeared to be much more sudden and abrupt than were expected by natural selection. He drew an analogy between what was happening at the population level and at the species level. Just as those individuals would be favored that could survive to maturity and also be capable of producing lots of offspring, species would be favored that had a lengthy existence in order to provide more opportunity for speciation and also for their tendency to produce many daughter species. In this analogy speciation was the analogue to birth and extinction to death. Thus a more accurate description would be species sorting rather than species selection.

A somewhat surprising consequence of these ideas was that chance events may play a much more important role in evolution than previously thought. The birth or extinction of species might be due more to the often arbitrary nature of climatic and geological changes. Rather than assuming the fossil record was poorly preserved, David Raup suggested that the patterns might be better understood if they were the result of stochastic or random rather than deterministic processes. He pioneered techniques that applied sophisticated statistical analysis to the fossil record and computer simulations to test this idea. He wrote a computer program that produced simulated phyletic trees with the likelihood of a particular lineage producing a new species or going extinct set at a randomly generated variable. This is known as a statistical random walk. The trees that resulted were virtually identical to what was observed in the fossil record. This did not prove that extinction and species origination were random processes, but it certainly challenged the idea that natural selection was the primary causative agent in shaping the broad patterns exhibited by the history of life. Raup became interested in the role of extinction and examined the fossil record for mass extinctions where up to 95 percent of existing taxa were wiped out in a relatively short period of time. His analysis suggested a periodicity to mass extinctions and they occurred at regular intervals of about 26 million years. Independently, at the same time Walter and Luis Alvarez claimed that a major extraterrestrial impact such as a meteorite had hit the earth at the boundary of the Cretaceous and Tertiary periods (65 mya) based on high levels of iridium along with other indicators of impact such as shocked quartz crystals found at the KT boundary (Cretaceous is spelled with a K in German). This was the time of the dinosaur extinction. This idea was initially highly controversial, but as more KT boundary sites were sampled that showed high iridium levels and evidence of a 150-kilometer-wide impact crater was located just off the Yucatán peninsula, it became well accepted. This fueled the discussion about the role of natural selection vs. chance events in shaping earth history. The dinosaurs were doing just fine until a meteorite crashed into the earth. While the basic process of natural selection adapts organisms to the environment, if a catastrophic change occurs it might not matter. Mammals already existed during the time of the dinosaurs, but they were very small rodent-like creatures. They might have remained so for several more millions of years. Instead, the demise of the dinosaurs opened up several niches that allowed the mammals to expand and ultimately made possible the rise of *Homo sapiens*. Interestingly, the rise of the dinosaurs might also be the consequence of a mass-extinction event. They made their first appearance in the fossil record in the Triassic about 230 mya, but for the first 30 million years they were only a small part of terrestrial animal communities. At the end of the Triassic another major extinction occurred and it was after that the dinosaurs rose to dominate the land for the next 150 million years. As Raup titled his popular book exploring these ideas, was it *Bad Genes or Bad Luck* that determined who survived and who didn't? Imagine a species that is the best-adapted fish with its superior fins and sleek design swimming in a pond, but if the pond dries up that species goes extinct. Another fish that might be rather poorly adapted for water with stubby feet-like fins and an air bladder that allowed it to extract oxygen from the air would be the species that started off an entirely new adaptive radiation, generating novel new structures. Yet it might literally never have gotten a toehold onto earth if the pond had not dried up.

The idea of periodicity has not really held up, but the approaches pioneered by Raup, Stanley and others have truly revolutionized the way paleontology is being taught and the approach to the fossil record. In addition to describing various fossils, computer analysis is routinely applied to vast data sets. It has shown the fossil record exhibits a variety of patterns: gradualism without stasis, gradualism with stasis or punctuation with stasis. This has stimulated research as to when and why particular patterns might prevail. If speciation were the result of reproductive isolation, then the frequency of it would be related to how easy reproductive barriers appear. At one extreme would be the example of the cichlids that live in an environment that has several micro-environments to exploit. At the other extreme are organisms such a planktonic protists that have enormous populations and seldom encounter any barriers to dispersal. Simple organisms, they also do not have the potential to evolve the elaborate reproductive behaviors of the cichlids. They have evolved slowly and individual species are relatively long lived. Yet other dynamics can operate as well. In a rapidly changing environment it might pay to not be highly specialized, but rather a generalist that can survive in many different kinds of environments. As the cichlids demonstrated, stable environments allow very specialized adaptations to eventually evolve.

The fossil record is imperfect and always will be. Paleontologists estimate that less than 1 percent of all species become fossilized. Nevertheless, it tells us a great deal about the history of life. It documents unequivocally that life has evolved and that **biodiversity** has steadily increased. Extinct groups show us the myriad of ways that life has solved problems of survival and reproduction, continuing to invent novel structures whether it was wings to fly or feet to walk on land. Fossils give us a view into a past inhabited by creatures so fantastic that as Cuvier wrote of the plesiosaur, they "astonished naturalists [and] without the slightest doubt would seem incredible to anyone who had not been able to observe them himself."

OF FEATHERED DINOSAURS, FISH WITH FEET, AND MISSING LINKS

Many fossils are often described as a "missing link." However, this is a highly problematic term. How big a gap does there need to be in the fossil record for something to count as a missing link? Each time a new fossil is discovered the gap will be lessened, but at what point would the gap be considered essentially closed? Proponents of ID (intelligent design) often use the term missing link as evidence for their point of view, quoting paleontologists out of context, distorting what was really meant. For example, fossil tetrapod footprints have been found in Poland that pre-date Tiktaalik by 10 million years. ID'ers claim that Tiktaalik can no longer be considered a missing link between fish and tetrapods because this is evidence that tetrapods existed that are older than Tiktaalik. The Discovery Institute claims this find "blows Tiktaalik out of the amazing that we have as good a record of transitional fossils or missing links as we do and we continue to find more and more every day.

ARCHETYPES, ANCESTORS AND EMBRYOS

Paleontologists had always been sympathetic to the anatomists' concept of the bauplan, the idea that a general blueprint or plan exists that describes the common and homologous features of a particular group or taxa. This was because the pattern of the fossil record suggests that evolution has involved elaboration of a relatively small number of combinations of major body parts. Paleontologists refer to the possible morphologies that organisms can occupy as morphospace. The fossil record documents that not all theoretically available morphospace is filled. For example, having wheels would be a great means of locomotion, but such a form has never evolved. Neither has something with four legs and four wings. Several explanations have been offered. Functionalists argue that the missing forms have been selected against. Historicists claim that a particular lineage is constrained historically and hasn't diffused sufficiently to fill the space. Contingency and chance, including the effect of mass extinctions, play a large role in their interpretation of the fossil record. However, another explanation suggests that certain forms have never evolved, because of developmental constraints that limit the possibilities. Not just any form can evolve, no matter how adaptive it might be, and a complete explanation for the pattern of the fossil record must draw on research from developmental biologists. The revitalization of paleontology combined with the research in molecular biology has resulted in what is now one of the most exciting areas in evolution studies: evolutionary developmental biology or "evo-devo," which seeks to obtain a full integration of embryology with evolution. The diversity of life that we observe today is a product of both **phylogeny** (the evolutionary history of the species) and **ontogeny** (the developmental history of an individual from the embryo to an adult).

EVOLUTIONARY DEVELOPMENTAL BIOLOGY

E. S. Russell (1887–1954) in his classic work *Form and Function* documented that one of the most fundamental debates in water." First, several paleontologists are not convinced that the footprints were made by a tetrapod, but even if they were, this is a totally specious argument. Evolution is not a ladder, but a bush with most branches or lineages eventually going extinct. We continue to find more and more transitional fossils that are filling in the branches of the bush. As more and more branches are discovered, it is consistently found that the origin of a particular group is much older than when it first makes its appearance in the record. Dinosaurs were dated as first appearing about 230 mya. Recently, a Tanzanian fossil dates the existence of dinosaurs to 243 million years. This is exactly what Darwin predicted and has been borne out. The term missing link was sometimes used to describe *Archaeopteryx* when it was first discovered because it had several reptile-like features. Yet it was classified as a bird just as Tiktaalik was classified as a fish. By definition neither of these two fossils are missing links between two groups because they are classified as belonging to a particular group. Many fossil birds are older than Archaeopteryx and like it virtually all of them became extinct. Assuming tetrapods made the footprints, all this means is that Tiktaalik is not in the lineage that gave rise to tetrapods, just as most bird-like dinosaurs did not evolve into birds. However, a particular lineage eventually evolved enough traits such as feathers to change its classification from dinosaur to bird. In the fossil record species can be identified only by their morphology and this also means that the classification of species is somewhat arbitrary. Tiktaalik remains a valuable fossil find because it exhibits traits that are transitional between aquatic and land-based organisms. We continue to find fossils that put us closer and closer to the branch point between various groups, more and more "missing links." As **Chapter 5** will show, we now have more and more fossil **hominids** that are ever closer to the branch point between humans and apes. How to classify them has caused heated controversies, based on highly technical discussions on partial remains. Nevertheless, our understanding of human evolution has become increasingly rich and complex. Yet given the nature of the fossil record, it is unrealistic to think that we will identify a fossil species and say this is IT. Some of its offspring gave rise to a lineage that eventually evolved into the great apes while a different subpopulation eventually became humans. This is true for virtually every transition. When the fossil record is looked at in this way, it is nineteenth-century biology was over what was primary: form or function. Although many developmentalists argued against Darwin's theory, they were not just misunderstanding the theory or tied to backward ideas. Rather, they raised issues that remained problematic throughout the twentieth century. Von Baer maintained that "usefulness" was an incomplete criterion for evolutionary change because, as he pointed out, there would have been many times in evolutionary history that having four legs and two wings would have been advantageous, yet such a form never evolved. He believed internal factors limited the types of variability produced that natural selection could act on. For von Baer, these constraints meant that natural selection could not account for the origin of his four distinct types from a single primeval germ.

Natural selection provided only a partial explanation to the question that most interested morphologists such as von Baer and Huxley: How does form come to be? Not only is development the key to understanding how a single cell becomes a complex, multi-billioncelled organism, but it is also thoroughly connected to evolution, since it is through changes in the embryo that changes in form arise. It is ironic that embryology was eclipsed with the rise of population genetics because it was always central to Darwin's thinking. For him, embryology provided the strongest evidence in favor of evolution, and the crucial concept in embryology was **homology**. He wrote Huxley, "I do not look at [homology] as mere analogy. I would as soon believe that fossil shells were mere mockeries of real shells as that the same bones in the foot of a dog and wing of a bat, or the similar embryo of mammal and bird, had not a direct signification, and the signification be unity of descent or nothing." Today homology is at the heart of research that is trying to fully incorporate the findings in development with evolutionary theory.

When we say that a mammalian hormone is the same as a fish hormone, that the human DNA sequence is the same as a sequence in a chimp or a mouse or that of yeast, or that fruit flies and frogs share many of the same genes as humans, we are making a direct statement about homology. Nevertheless, defining homology has always been somewhat problematic. Darwin claimed that the "essential" similarities observed between different organisms were the result of having a common ancestry. After Darwin an interesting and not uncommon transition took place: from explanation to definition. Instead of homology being evidence for evolution and a phylogenetic relationship, it became part of the definition. Homology was defined as any similarity that could be traced to ancestry. However, similar structures often arise independently; and in contrast, often very different structures arise through evolutionary transformation. In determining genealogies one has to rely in large part on similarity of character. One has to make a choice as to which should be given primacy – similarity or ancestry. Homology was being used to explain both the maintenance of similarity and the transformation of form.

The key to homology was to understand its genetic under-pinnings. At the end of the nineteenth century William Bateson catalogued a variety of "monsters," aberrant forms that displayed extra, missing, or altered parts. Those mutants in which one body part was transformed into another he called **homeotic** (from the Greek *homeos* meaning same or similar). As the fruit fly became the organism of choice for genetic experiments, geneticists isolated several different homeotic flies. For example, in the *bithorax* mutant the normally tiny hindwings looked like the much larger forewings. Antennapedia caused legs to appear instead of antennae on the head. These dramatic effects were under the control of single genes. In the past 20 years biologists have worked out the details of how these homeotic mutants are created. *Hox* "master" genes shape the development of body regions along the body axis of the fly. *Hox* genes belong to a class of genes that share a short, virtually identical sequence of DNA that geneticists named the homeobox. The discovery of the homeobox created havoc with the traditional distinction between homology and analogy because "homologous" genes are responsible for "analogous" processes, i.e what have always been regarded as examples of **convergent evolution** have the same genetic underpinnings. The segmentation in the body parts of flies and vertebrates was always cited as a classic example of analogy, but *Hox* genes have been conserved through over 500 million years of evolutionary history. The same genes were found in various insects, earthworms, frogs, mice, and even humans. The *Hox* genes in mice were arranged in clusters just as they were in the fly, and the order corresponded to the order of the body regions in the mouse in which they were expressed, just as they were in flies.

The vertebrate and the insect eye were also regarded as analogous structures. However, they are both based on the expression of the *Pax*-6 gene. Along with cephalopod eyes they are all descendants of a basic metazoan photoreceptor cell that was regulated by the *Pax*-6 gene.

Flies do not have much of a heart by vertebrate standards, but they do contain a structure along the topside of their body that pumps fluids along the inside of the body. They have an open circulation system, meaning the blood just bathes the tissues and is not compartmentalized. Geneticists isolated a gene they named *tinman* (after the Tin Man who didn't have a heart from *The Wizard of Oz*) that was needed to make the heart. Several mammalian versions of the *tinman* gene have been isolated that belong to the NK2 family, which plays an important role in the development of the heart. In spite of the enormous differences between the heart and circulatory system of flies and humans, a similar gene is responsible for the formation and patterning of their hearts. Several different families of homeobox genes have been discovered, which all have dramatic effects on the formation of body parts. By binding to specific regions of DNA we know they turn genes either on or off in developing limbs, eyes, and heart respectively. They have such large effects because they either regulate large numbers of genes, or act early on in development, or both. These examples along with many others have resulted in a revisiting of the meaning of homology. Homology has traditionally been associated with structure, but the discovery of these homologous genes of process is at the core of understanding development. The discovery that the same set of genes controls the formation of body regions and body parts in organisms as diverse as fruit flies, frogs, and zebras has resulted in a complete rethinking of animal history, the origins of structure, and the nature of diversity.

Ever since Darwin, a persistent question has been the one that Huxley first raised when he wondered whether natural selection had the power to create new species rather than just well-marked varieties. How is novelty created? The astounding findings of the past 30 years have shown us that the creation of new forms is possible because of a few key concepts. First, evolution works by tinkering with what is already present. Wings did not spring *de novo* from a four-legged vertebrate. Second, structures can have a variety of functions. Wing structures were probably not originally used for flying, but for thermoregulation. Multifunctionality extends to the level of the gene, with the same "old" gene being used in many different ways. Third is the idea of redundancy. Simply duplicating a particular structure can generate very different forms. Any part of a multifunctional structure that is even partially redundant in function sets the stage for specialization through the division of labor that eventually results in the structure differing both in form and function from the original. Gene duplication has been an important source of innovation, making it possible for the same gene to be used in many different ways. Finally, modularity has been crucial to the creation of an enormous amount of diversity. Through duplication, mixing, and modification of various parts, arthropods have evolved different structures with different functions from the same basic unit, leading to the most diverse group of animals on earth. The modular nature of digits made possible the evolution of a long fourth finger in pterosaurs and many long fingers in bats on which to extend a wing membrane.

Millions of antibodies can be coded for with relatively few genes because of the modularity of their structure. The key to this diversity is the modular genetic logic of the switches in development, allowing one part of a structure to be modified independently of another. The fossil record documents a Cambrian "explosion," a burst of new forms never seen before. Today research in evo-devo is showing us that from a few basic building blocks, nature evolved the fundamental types of animals and body parts in the Cambrian that are found in present-day organisms. Yet from those basic forms an enormous amount of diversity continues to be generated in response to the ever-changing environment.

The complete unification of evolution with development is a work in progress that is being approached on several different fronts. Evolutionary changes in development must begin with variation within populations, but relatively little research has specifically examined this question. Some studies have examined genetic variations in the coding and regulatory sequences of developmental regulatory genes. Some comparisons among closely related species with distinct life histories or among populations that have distinct morphologies also can show how specific developmental mechanisms respond to changes in selection. Several very basic questions remain. First, what kind of genetic variation plays a role in evolutionary changes in development? In general, the large-scale mutations that Goldschmidt proposed are probably not a good model. Although on occasion such a mutation affects a regulatory gene that results in a dramatic change in phenotype that is viable, in general such phenotypes are rarely well integrated in terms of overall functionality. Many are probably lethal. Second, how much genetic variation in natural populations influences development? We know an enormous amount of variation exists and also that it affects gene expression, but demonstrating a direct connection between differences in gene expression and different phenotypes is difficult. Molecular and quantitative genetics are beginning to be able to answer this question. Third, one of the most interesting questions that has been raised by the accumulating data on homology of process is how do we square the lack of morphological intermediates with the idea that many developmental genes are conserved across all **phyla**, even across more than one kingdom. Conversely why can the activity of many different genes still generate similar structures? The unity of type that was embodied in von Baer's famous laws of development now has support in the detailed studies of molecular genetics, but a theoretical debate rages as to the meaning of these findings. Is the conservation of developmental pathways the result of selection or is it a property of generic systems that, in fact, is impervious to selection? Strict adaptationists argue that such conservation occurs because the optimality of these pathways has been reached and can't be improved upon. Yet some developmental biologists argue that developmental pathways limit what is possible. One of the most provocative researchers and advocate of a strong structural approach to this problem was Brian Goodwin (1931–2009) who examined the influences that affect the spatial order that emerges from cell–cell interactions. He and his collaborators explored the development of characteristic structures known as whorls in the life cycle of a particular alga and the family it belonged to. Although a great deal of variety existed in the shape of whorls between species and in a single whorl as the individual alga matured, they still represented variations on a theme that gives the entire group its taxonomic unity. According to Goodwin, organisms form natural groups not because of their history, but rather because of the way their basic structure is generated. Natural selection may only filter unsuccessful morphologies generated by development. The taxonomies that we have developed to describe the relationship of organisms to one another are not the result of trial and error tinkering by natural selection, but rather reflect a deep pattern of ordered relationships. Ever since Darwin, history has been intrinsic to our definition of homology and thus, Goodwin's repudiation of history in trying to discover the laws of form was quite radical. Furthermore, he thought natural selection does not inform the design of experiments in any significant way in trying to answer these fundamental questions regarding the nature of form. Instead, what was needed was a theory of morphogenesis, which would not be supplemental, but as fundamental to biology as the principle of natural selection. Even among developmental biologists sympathetic to a structural approach, Goodwin's position is regarded as extreme. Nevertheless, he has been an important thinker in regard to investigating this topic.

Another approach to integrating evolution with development is the field of ecological developmental evolutionary biology. As Leigh van Valen wrote "evolution is the control of development by ecology." It has been well known that several alternative developmental pathways exist to produce a particular structure, but they still give the same end result. This process is called canalization, described first by Conrad Waddington (1905–75). He suggested that natural selection created these pathways as a buffer again external perturbations such as unfavorable temperature and internal ones such as mutations to ensure normal development. For example, several species may reproduce either asexually or sexually and the adults are indistinguishable. At the same time development is not completely hard-wired, in that depending on environmental conditions different pathways may be chosen resulting in different phenotypes. Sometimes this might be a by-product of environmental perturbations that were not protected by canalization. In other cases it is a response to the environment and is clearly adaptive. Nevertheless, the evolutionary origin and basis of phenotypic plasticity remains poorly understood and varies tremendously from species to species. Think about the enormous variation that has been achieved in the breeding of domestic dogs, from Chihuahuas to Great Danes compared to cats, that show a much more limited range of size and shape. Is this plasticity the result of selection or the by-product of selection, i.e. are there specific "plasticity" genes? In some crocodiles and turtles sex determination is dependent on temperature and in some fish it depends on the social contexts. If many genes are sensitive to environmental cues then it is not necessary to posit specific "plasticity" genes. Differences in gene expression can cause differences in development, for example the various castes in bees and ants. Changes in gene expression may be as important as those in gene function to promote plasticity.

No one disputes the power of natural selection to cause adaptation, i.e. to shape organisms' form and function in order to maximize reproductive success. However, research on a variety of different fronts from paleontology to developmental biology brings into question whether natural selection provides a complete explanation for the history of life and the diversity of forms. Are micro-evolutionary changes in gene frequency all that is needed to turn a reptile into a mammal or a fish into an amphibian? Furthermore, it is not at all apparent that either homology or diversity are fundamentally adaptive phenomena. Because of the success of natural selection theory in explaining adaptive complexity in the twentieth century, the functionalist approach has been regarded as the more powerful. However, the idea of type provided a crucial organizing principle, led to the concept of homology, and as Darwin realized, could be used as evidence for his theory of common descent. Clearly the functional approach has been a powerful one, but it is also apparent that it still has not adequately answered profound questions relating to the nature of form. However, this should not be interpreted as evolution being discredited. Rather, it demonstrates that like all good scientific theories evolution continues to generate new questions and new approaches to answering old ones. The linking of development and evolution has benefited both disciplines. Phylogenetic methods have revealed that all **eukaryotes** share a "tool kit" of proteins that regulate developmental processes and these methods are now routinely used to describe developmental gene networks. Evolutionary biologists are incorporating the insights from development in their understanding of the relationship between genotype and phenotype. Instead of abstract models of single loci they are now modeling gene networks based on real organisms. This partnership holds the promise of understanding both the pattern and process of evolution at the most fundamental level.

FURTHER READING

Ayala, F. (2009) "Molecular evolution," in M. Ruse and J. Travis (eds) *Evolution: The First Four Billion Years,* Cambridge, MA: Belknap Press.

Benton, M. (2009) "Paleontology and the history of life," in M. Ruse and J. Travis (eds) *Evolution: The First Four Billion Years,* Cambridge, MA: Belknap Press.

Caroll, S. (2006) *Endless Forms Most Beautiful: The New Science of Evo Devo,* New York: W. W. Norton.

Prothero. D. (1992) "Punctuated equilibrium at twenty: a paleontological perspective," *Skeptic* 1(3): 38–47.

Weiner, J. (1994) *The Beak of the Finch,* New York: Vintage Press.

Wray, G. (2009) "Evolution and Development," in M. Ruse and J. Travis (eds) *Evolution: The First Four Billion Years,* Cambridge, MA: Belknap Press.

WEBSITES

Evolution Today: How does natural selection work bib.amnh.org/exhibitions/darwin/evolution/ancient.php

Nuts and Bolts of DNA Replication bib.pbs.org/wgbh/evolution/library/06/3/l_063_02.html

Punctuated equilibrium bib.pbs.org/wgbh/evolution/library/03/5/l_035_01.html

Unofficial SJG Archive: Library bib.stephenjaygould.org/library.html

5

HUMAN EVOLUTION

HUMANKIND'S PLACE IN NATURE

Where we come from is a question that has occupied humankind from the time our ancestors had brains big enough to contemplate such questions. While numerous controversies have surrounded evolutionary theory from Darwin's time to the present, the ones that have garnered the most attention concern claims that have been made in regard to humans, specifically about our nature. Although Darwin did not think humans were an exception to evolution, he was initially reluctant to elaborate on how his theory applied to humans. He knew that any discussion of human evolution would become emotionally charged and highly politicized. This was true in Victorian times and remains so today. Throughout the twentieth century more and more fossils were discovered, pushing human origins further and further back in time and documenting that humans were no exception to Darwin's theory. We now have a rich fossil record that is filling in the branches of the human tree. Today, advances in molecular genetics are allowing us to trace the lineage of anatomically modern humans in great detail. DNA has even been extracted from Neanderthal bones. Research in animal behavior also demonstrates continuity between animal and human minds. The evidence in favor of human evolution is overwhelming. However, evidence must be interpreted. Dating of remains is often problematical and rarely is anything even close to a complete skeleton found. Experts disagree as to whether certain fossils represent two different species, whether they should be categorized as two different genera, or merely represent sexual dimorphism within a single species. We cannot do experiments that recreate the past. Perhaps most important, behavior does not fossilize. The attempt to build an evolutionary theory of human nature dramatically illustrates the large role interpretation plays in determining the "facts" of human evolution. Facts only have meaning within a theoretical framework and the various theories that have been constructed have been loaded with the cultural values of the researchers. This is true of all science, but has especially plagued the field of human origins where gender, race, and nationalism have significantly influenced the construction of a theory. Because of these problems, it is not inappropriate to refer to theories about human origins as stories. This is not meant in a pejorative sense or to downplay the immense amount of work that has been done in a variety of disciplines from molecular biology to archeology to primatology. This story aspect of human origins is not something that can be gotten rid of by better methodology – that is by better quantitative analysis or higher standards for fieldwork. Obviously, improved methods never hurt any endeavor, but a major aspect of human evolutionary theory has been the actual construction of good stories. All stories are not equally good and the stories that are told are intimately linked with the questions that are asked, which in turn are a reflection of the sources of power, the intertwining of sex, race, and class of the researchers, and of the countries where the fieldwork is done. For example, the notorious Piltdown man found in Sussex, England, by amateur geologist Charles Dawson in 1912 was regarded as one of our earliest ancestors for almost half a century. It was finally exposed as a hoax in 1953 when Kenneth Oakley demonstrated unequivocally that the remains were a human cranium and an orang-utan jaw, both of which had been artificially stained. The hoax was perpetuated for as long as it was because it fit into the researchers preconceived biases, which in turn were a reflection of their race, and country of origin. Piltdown man was big brained and found not in Africa, home of "savages," or even Asia, which was slightly more suitable, but in England. Yet it is important to recognize that the fraud was finally exposed, in no small part due to the fact that Piltdown man was becoming an increasingly anomalous fossil in relation to the other fossils that were being discovered in Asia and Africa. Evidence *does* matter. Continued research has contributed to a better, more coherent, fuller story of our origins, and what it means to be human or animal. It has provided us with a more accurate description of humans and how we differ from apes and monkeys. The controversies that surround human evolution do not mean that the evidence for evolution is weak, but rather that the process of science is working just the way it should be.

CONVINCING MEN THEY ARE MONKEYS

Many people were willing to accept Darwin's theory for the animal and plant kingdom, but they exempted humans as special. As scientists argued whether natural selection could account for species change, whether change was gradual or saltational, and a myriad of other aspects of Darwin's theory, these issues were not the basis for the fundamental objection to *The Origin*. Rather, opponents claimed it was a materialistic, atheistic doctrine. Particularly upsetting were the implications for human origins. Darwin was telling Victorians that rather than being made in God's image, humans were little more than intelligent apes.

Unlike Darwin who avoided controversy and did not like being in the public eye, Huxley thrived on conflict and wrote Darwin "I am sharpening my claws and beak in readiness." In a famous encounter at the British Association for the Advancement of Science meetings at Oxford in 1860, Huxley was asked by Bishop Wilberforce (known as Soapy Sam), who had been coached by Richard Owen, whether "it was on his grandfather's or his grandmother's side that the ape ancestry comes in." Huxley replied "that a man has no reason to be ashamed of having an ape for his grandfather. ... Rather, he would be more ashamed of having an ancestor who had no real knowledge of the scientific issues and chose to obscure them by aimless rhetoric and appeals to religious prejudice." Claiming one would rather be related to an ape than a bishop created quite a stir. According to one account a lady fainted. Huxley decided to devote his weekly lectures to workingmen to "The Relationship of Men to the Rest of the Animal Kingdom." The lectures were quite popular, and he quipped to his wife, "By next

Friday evening they will all be convinced they are monkeys."
Refined and expanded, they eventually became part of *Man's Place
in Nature* (1863) providing a variety of different kinds of evidence
that humans were no exception to evolutionary theory. Rather
than asking whether humans were descended from an ape-like
ancestor, instead Huxley asked what was the relationship of humans
to other primates, approaching the question just as a taxonomist
would investigate how closely related were the cat and the dog.
The classification of humans ran the whole gamut from being classified as a primate along with apes and monkeys, to being thought
so special that they deserved their own separate kingdom. Huxley
presented evidence from comparative anatomy and embryology
that demonstrated the differences between humans and the higher
apes (gorillas, chimpanzees and orang-utans) were no greater than
those between the higher and lower apes (monkeys). See **Figure 5.1**.
If Darwin's hypothesis explained the common ancestry of the
higher and lower apes, then it followed that it also explained the
shared origin of the higher apes with humans. Not only was there a
similarity in anatomical structures, but animals also shared certain
mental attributes with humans. Cats and dogs responded to our
emotions in kind, hatred with hatred, love with love. They exhibited sorrow and shame. The evidence for our common shared
ancestry was overwhelming. Yet beliefs run deep and many people
still thought accepting such an idea would result in the brutalization

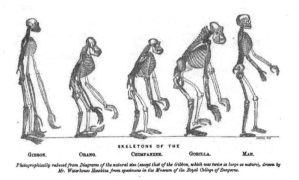

Figure 5.1 Thomas Huxley's *Man's Place in Nature*

and loss of dignity for humans. Many people think this today and Huxley's words remain relevant.

> Is it, indeed, true, that the Poet, or the Philosopher, or the Artist whose genius is the glory of his age, is degraded from his high estate by the undoubted historical probability, not to say certainty, that he is the direct descendant of some naked and bestial savage. ... Is mother-love vile because a hen shows it, or fidelity base because dogs possess it?
>
> ([1863] 1898: 152–54)

Just because we share admirable traits with the lower animals does not make these traits less admirable. Only humans were capable of intelligible and rational speech that made possible the development of culture and civilization. Even if humans came *from* the brutes, they were not *of* them.

Fossils provided another kind of evidence that argued for the common ancestry between apes and humans. The first Neanderthal fossils were discovered shortly before the publication of *The Origin*. However, these ancient bones were not significantly different from modern humans and thus they did not represent a missing link that connected humans to apes. Huxley correctly anticipated that the finds of paleontology would push the origin of humans back to a far earlier epoch than anyone had previously imagined. If humankind was that ancient, this was evidence against the creation hypothesis. The Darwinian hypothesis was the only hypothesis that could make sense of these ancient human fossils.

Not only did Darwin's theory ignite controversy about the origin of all humankind, but it also rekindled the eighteenth-century debate over the origin of the different human races. Were human races separate species (polygenesis) or just varieties of a single species (**monogenesis**)? In light of evolution the question became, "Were present day human races derived from distinct species of ape-like ancestors or just varieties that developed later from one common ancestor?" In 1864 Wallace put forth a theory that was compatible with the two different hypotheses. It also explained why the human body with the exception of the skull looked so similar to the bodies of the present-day apes, while at the same time the skull and mental abilities diverged widely from these same apes. He suggested that humans, unlike other organisms, had experienced two distinct stages in evolution. In the first stage, human ancestors had evolved just as any other creature according to the principle of natural selection. Thus, individuals who carried favorable variations in the constant struggle for existence survived, their form continuing to be modified. But once the human brain had evolved to a certain point and the moral and intellectual capabilities were fairly well developed, natural selection would no longer act on the human physical form and structure, and it would remain essentially unchanged. Humans were able to adapt to harsh and changing environmental conditions by the use of their intellect alone. Animals might develop a thick coat of fur or a layer of fat if the climate became colder, but humans would put on warmer clothes and build a shelter. No change in body structure would be required. Early on humans developed hunting techniques that did not rely so much on their body. The use of fire made many new foods edible. Agriculture and the domestication of various animals also vastly increased the amount of food. By intellect alone, with no change in the body, humans could survive and adapt to the ever-changing environmental conditions. They developed social and sympathetic feelings that allowed them to band together for mutual comfort and protection, and such traits would be preserved and accumulated. Wallace claimed that the more intellectual and moral races would replace the lower ones. Such views also suggested that the human lineage must have first arisen when the brain size was still fairly small, at a far earlier time than most people thought, and when natural selection would still be acting on the body. Once the brain had reached a certain level of development, it protected the body from the action of natural selection and prevented any further racial divergence. Only the mind continued to evolve. This last point also addressed the real question that underlay the debate, which was not a scientific one about human origins, but a more insidious one regarding the intellectual and moral qualities of the different races. If each race had a separate origin, then they were in reality different species. From there it was a small step to claim that some races were superior to others, which in turn was used to justify slavery, imperialism, and various racial theories. Monogenists in arguing for a single origin of all human beings claimed that they had scientific proof that the "savage" races were not qualitatively different or inferior to their masters or colonial administrators. Abolitionists and members of other humanitarian reform movements used the monogenist position to further their own goals. Darwin definitely wanted to use his theory to argue against slavery. Wallace's ingenious solution to this controversy essentially amounted to a moral monogenesis and a physical polygenesis. He claimed that early humans were a single homogenous race. At that time, our ancestors had a human form, but did not yet have a well-developed brain. They did not have speech or the sympathetic and moral feelings characteristic of modern humans. If one did not consider these ancestors to be fully human until the higher faculties were fairly well developed, then one could assert that there were many distinct races of humans. However, if one thought that our ancestors whose form was essentially modern, but whose mental faculties were scarcely raised above the brute, still deserved to be considered fully human, then all of humankind shared a common origin. Thus, Wallace did not deny that physical and racial differences existed, which could have been due to separate origins, but that all depended on how one defined the origin of the human species. The different races all had evolved to a certain point at which they all exhibited a shared common humanity. If one defined the origin of the human species at that point in time, then the different races represented variants of a single species. Wallace was in many ways ahead of his time in recognizing that our ancestors were small brained and quite ape-like. He was also remarkably free of the prevailing racist attitudes of his contemporaries regarding native peoples. Darwin had been very impressed with Wallace's ideas about human evolution and offered to give him his notes on man, claiming his own thoughts on the matter were in a state of chaos, but Wallace declined the offer.

THE HARDEST CASE: THE MORAL SENSE

After the publication of *The Origin*, research continued to narrow the gap between humans and animals. Fossil evidence, comparative anatomy and molecular evidence all document how close we are to our primate cousins. Characteristics that were supposedly unique to humans, such as language and tool use, have also been observed in chimps and other animals. Even in Darwin's time evidence was available that showed the difference between human and animal intelligence was one of degree rather than kind. Nevertheless, people continued to maintain that an unbridgeable gap existed between humans and animals. Much to Darwin's dismay, in 1869 Wallace did a dramatic turn about, and came to think that natural selection could not account for various traits such as the hand, the loss of hair, and the organs of speech. Why would prehistoric man need such a big brain? Most important, how could a sense of morality have evolved? Much to everyone's surprise, Wallace claimed that a higher power was guiding the action of natural selection for special ends. Many people have claimed that Wallace changed his mind because of his involvement with spiritualism. Wallace had certainly been influenced by spiritualism, but the answer is much more complex. One could argue that he was even more of a selectionist than Darwin as he insisted this was not a negation of the principle of natural selection. Rather, just as humans selected particular variations to produce desirable varieties of fruits, vegetables, and livestock, an "overruling intelligence" had watched over the action of laws of variation and selection, resulting in the advancement of the mental and moral capabilities of humans. Wallace made no reference to spiritualism and grounded his argument in utility alone. As Darwin emphasized and Wallace agreed, natural selection would not preserve a structure that would be valuable for future generations nor would favorable variations accumulate to provide a more perfect structure if a less efficient one could do the job in the continual struggle for survival. Wallace had lived with native peoples for extended periods of time in the Amazon and recognized that the "savage" races were no different than "civilized" Victorian gentlemen. They were just as intelligent, had the same moral capabilities, and the same range of emotions. He thought this would have been true for the prehistoric races as well. Yet he thought they had no need for such traits under the conditions in which they lived. Thus natural selection would produce a man with a brain "a little superior to that of an ape whereas he actually possesses one very little inferior to that of a philosopher." They had mathematical ability, ability to form abstract ideas, ability to perform complex trains of reasoning, aesthetic qualities, and high moral qualities, but these abilities were rarely used. Wallace even doubted whether civilized man made full use of these capabilities. He concluded that they were for the use of civilized man's future, not just for prehistoric man's future. The most difficult trait was conscience, the development of a moral sense. Although he thought that cooperation could be adaptive, the complex moral behavior of humans could not just be reduced to cooperation and seemed to be totally inexplicable on the grounds of utility alone. However, morality was an essential part of human nature. Even if selection were capable of producing the beginnings of human reason and the moral sentiment, intensified social and sympathetic feelings would prevent the beneficial culling of the mentally and morally inferior. Therefore, natural selection would become disengaged. For Wallace, the essence of human beings was that they were spiritual beings and this is what provided the basis for ethical and moral behavior. Wallace insisted this idea of a guiding force did not negate the importance of natural selection, but rather was an extension to providing a complete account of the history of life.

Wallace was not some ignorant fundamentalist, but someone who had independently co-discovered the principle of natural selection. Regardless of the influence of spiritualism on his views, his arguments as to the inadequacy of natural selection to account for particular traits were serious ones that Darwin needed to address. Darwin might have wanted to avoid dealing with human evolution, but this was the question that was on everyone's minds – not just Wallace's. Lyell had also maintained that humans were the exception to the general evolutionary process. In *Man's Place in Nature*, Huxley had made a powerful case for our shared ancestry with the apes, but he had not addressed the problem of the evolution of morality. Darwin needed to show that humans were no exception to his theory. In 1871 in *The Descent of Man and Selection in Relation to Sex* Darwin presented a theory of how the moral sense could have evolved. Just as Huxley had done in *Man's Place in Nature,* Darwin used comparative anatomy and embryology to demonstrate how similar humans were to apes. In *The Origin*, he had argued that homologous anatomical structures in humans and animals suggested they shared a common ancestor. He continued this same line of reasoning in *Descent*, but in addition he focused on homologous mental attributes. Basic emotions such as courage, fear, affection, shame, and fundamental mental faculties such as imitation, imagination, and reason were possessed by animals as well as by humans. The grief female monkeys expressed for the loss of their offspring, the curiosity of young apes, the jealousy and shame of dogs, and the reasoning abilities of higher animals all illustrated our shared intellectual and emotional heritage with the lower animals. Even traits that were considered unique to humans such as the ability to use tools, language, and an aesthetic sense existed to some degree in the lower animals. Apes manipulated sticks and pebbles for a variety of purposes. A species of Galapagos finch used a cactus spine to dig for insects. Animals might not have symbolic language, but they certainly were able to communicate information, some of which was quite complex. Male birds elaborately displayed their plumes and splendid colors before female birds just as women decorated their hats with brightly colored feathers. Natural theologians used similar examples to support the argument from design, but Darwin used them to tell a very different story: how the moral sense could have evolved. Specifically Darwin presented a theory of conscience.

Darwin made an assumption in interpreting the behavior of animals that researchers continue to make today, in spite of the risks associated with it. Yet it is a key aspect of attributing a particular mental state to an animal. Since the brain and nervous system of animals were similarly organized to our own, if an animal exhibited a particular behavior that had a human counterpart Darwin reasoned that the underlying psychic state was similar as well. If Cassie asked Grahame to bring her a copy of *Evolution: The Basics* and he does, she assumes that he understood her. If she said, "Fetch" to a dog and he brings her the paper we assume at least at some level the dog understood her. When Cassie pets her cat to show her affection and the cat likewise rubs and nuzzles her, most of us would interpret that to mean that the cat is showing her affection as well. When we don't even know what our fellow human beings are thinking most of the time, how can we really know what the underlying mental state of an animal is? Nevertheless, we make judgments all the time about the mental states of both people and animals based on their behavior. We have learned a great deal about both animal and human mental life using this principle of psychological attribution, in spite of making mistakes as well. This principle was a crucial part of Darwin's evidence for his theory of conscience that consisted of four overlapping stages, and which he saw as the basis of morality.

First, organisms developed a social instinct causing them to take pleasure in the company of others and bond together as closely related and associated individuals into society. The first social bond to evolve was undoubtedly between mother and offspring. In the second stage, animals evolved sufficient intellect to recall instances when the social instincts such as feeding one's offspring went unsatisfied in order to satisfy stronger urges such as hunger or sexual drive. Memory was a crucial aspect of intelligence. A mother might have abandoned her baby in search of food, but if she remembered that she did so, this would set up a conflict between different urges and could become the basis of a conscience. In highly developed organisms such as ourselves, often these more basic urges would be sacrificed to satisfy the well-developed social instincts, such as when one gives up one's own life to save a drowning child. The development of language in the third stage enabled early humans to become sensitized to mutual needs and to codify principles of their behavior. Finally, habit would come to shape the conduct of individuals so that even concerning small matters, acting in light of the wishes of the community would become, in a sense, second nature. Darwin saw these as sequential, but overlapping stages and devoted most of his energy into the first two. He provided numerous illustrations of the social instincts in action. Rabbits stamping their feet in warning, old crows feeding their companions who were blind, an old baboon heroically rescuing an infant attacked by dogs, were all examples of helping and protective behavior suggesting that animals expressed sympathy in some sort of rudimentary form. In addition, Darwin differed from the prevailing view of most British moral theorists and psychologists at the time who claimed that sympathy was a learned behavior in response to pleasure and pain. Cassie showed sympathy for Grahame when he slammed his finger in the door because Cassie had also slammed her finger and could recall that sense of pain that made her empathize with Grahame. Darwin rejected this analysis, instead arguing that social and sympathetic reactions were instinctive, not learned, and provided many examples of these behaviors in animals. Darwin claimed that if social and altruistic behavior was instinctive, it was highly probable that an animal that had well-developed social instincts would inevitably acquire a moral sense or conscience as soon as its intellectual powers approached that of humans. However, social instincts alone were not enough to form what would be considered conscience or a moral sense and an important difference existed between our behavior and that of animals. An evolved intellect played two important roles. First, reason and experience would guide conduct that had been stimulated by the social instincts. Although no specific instincts existed to tell one how to aid a fellow human being, the impulse to aid *was* instinctive. One learned how to give aid by observing the actions of members of the community. With the evolution of speech moral behavior would become more routine, reinforced by the language of praise and blame. Second, memory allowed one to compare past and future actions or motives, approving or disapproving of them. Darwin argued that conscience and moral obligation arose from the persistent social instincts. He did not deny that a huge difference between animals and humans existed. Dogs could not be considered fully moral beings because they did not have the ability to reflect on their behavior and re-establish a suppressed social instinct. However, the importance in Darwin's thinking is not just that he showed how having a conscience could be useful and therefore selected for, but also that the beginnings of the moral sense could be seen in animals. Research in both animal and human behavior has continued to build on his fundamental insights and has also overwhelmingly shown that there is a continuum between instinctive and learned behavior in both humans and animals. If we define morality as right and wrong behaviors in the context of the rules of a social group and ethics as the scientific study of, and theories about, moral thoughts and behaviors of a social group, is it possible to build a naturalistic ethics based on evolutionary theory? Evolutionary ethics has been plagued by all kinds of problems ever since Herbert Spencer coined the phrase "survival of the fittest." However, **Chapter 7** examines new research on the brain that suggests not only that evolution produced a species with a moral sense, but also that nature can provide guidance in defining right and wrong behavior.

THE FOSSIL EVIDENCE

Stephen Gould once said that he threw out his notes each year and started afresh in preparing his lectures on the fossil evidence for human evolution. The extreme rarity of hominid fossils meant that each new fossil often caused a dramatic reassessment and frequently precipitated major controversies. Nevertheless, several major discoveries in the past 20 years have greatly expanded our understanding and have confirmed the broad outlines that have been in place for the past 50 years of the major transitions from a small-brained ape-like creature to modern *Homo sapiens*. Once Darwin's theory was generally accepted, the question of human origins shifted. Instead of "Did we evolve from an ape-like creature?" the question became "How and when did we diverge from our ape-like ancestor?" Who was that ancestor and what was it like? In spite of this shift, many of the early theories espoused were still imbued with various emotional prejudices. Most people wanted our first ancestors to be as far back in time as possible, to maximize the distance between the brutish apes and modern humans. Other people, as mentioned, favored theories of multiple origins for humankind, which reflected the prevailing racist attitudes of the time. In 1891 Eugene Dubois found a skull and thigh bone in Java that were much more primitive than Neanderthal. Naming the fossil *Pithecanthropus erectus* (later *Homo erectus*), many thought it represented the missing link between apes and humans. Called Java man, it was also significant because it confirmed what Darwin had predicted: upright posture was acquired while the brain size was still essentially like that of an ape. In 1925 Raymond Dart discovered a fossil at Taung, a limestone quarry at the edge of the Transvaal in South Africa, which appeared to be intermediate between humans and chimpanzees. The fossil was a juvenile and became known as the Taung child. Dart named it *Australopithecus africanus*, but it was often disparagingly referred to as Dart's ape. It came from the wrong country – Africa, not Asia, and something that was so ape-like with its small brain could not possibly be on the road to humanity. At the time it was the earliest hominid found anywhere, but the "experts" decided that it was an interesting and peculiarly specialized southern off-shoot of the gorilla–chimpanzee stock, which showed some convergences with hominids, but it was not relevant to human origins. Instead, paleoanthropologists continued to be influenced by the fossil that misled them for almost half a century, *Eoanthropus dawsoni* the notorious Piltdown man. It played a prominent role in the reluctance of paleoanthropologists to accept the Taung child as part of the **Hominidae**, in spite of the fact that its teeth appeared to be more human-like than those of Piltdown man. Once it was exposed for the fake that it was, the fossils from Africa were looked at in a different light. The discovery of hip bones showed that australopithecine walked upright. Dart's ape along with the other australopithecines were finally accepted into the human family in spite of their small brains. A major shift occurred in the evolutionary story that was being told about human ancestry as the meaning of hominid changed. Walking upright became the crucial defining characteristic of the human line, not having a big brain.

Until relatively recently the hominid fossil record was quite poor and this also made interpretation quite difficult. From the pioneering work of Louis and Mary Leakey in the 1950s and 1960s and their son Richard, Donald Johanson, and Tim White in the 1970s, a general scheme emerged in spite of some contentious debates over the interpretation of particular fossils. Several different species of australopithecines continue to be discovered, along with many different species within the genus of *Homo*. Anatomically modern humans have been found that are far older than previously thought. Astounding fossil finds along with improved genetic analysis cause a continuing editing of the story of our origins and our relationship to the great apes. Linnaeus classified humans, chimpanzees and orang-utans in the genus *Homo* (gorillas were not known at the time). They were grouped in the order he named Primate, which also included two other genera, simians and lemurs. In 1910 William King Gregory's reclassification put the great apes into their own family Pongidae and humans in the family Hominidae. However, genetic analysis suggested a different relationship that most comparative anatomists were initially quite resistant to. It showed that the African apes (gorillas and chimpanzees) were more similar to humans than they were to the Asian orang-utan. Monkeys were far more distantly related. Although quite controversial, improved immunological methods, DNA hybridization experiments, and a variety of different tools all have confirmed this relationship. Our classification has changed to reflect the true genetic relationships of these different species. The Asian apes and their ancestors are in the family Pongidae while the African apes are in the family Hominidae. This family now includes three subfamilies, Gorrilliane (gorilla), Panninae (bonobos and chimpanzees) and **Homininae** also referred to as hominid, or hominin (humans).

Molecular data puts the divergence between Homininae from the other groups in the Hominidae family at somewhere between 10 and 5 mya (million years ago). Not everyone agrees on how some of these oldest fossils should be classified. The oldest potential candidate to be classified as a hominid is *Sahelanthropus tchadensis,* based on a skull found in Chad, and is dated to be between 6 and 7 million years old. It is quite ape-like with an estimated brain capacity smaller than that of a chimpanzee. The foramen magnum (the opening at the base of the cranium through which the spinal cord passes) is further forward than in modern apes and is suggestive of upright posture. Another key feature that is used to define the exclusively hominid line is teeth. Reduction in the canines occurred, but the reasons for it are highly debated. Walking upright that freed the hand to fight and hold weapons, changes in mating systems and changes in diet have all been suggested as possible explanations. Both the size and pattern of wear of *S. tchadensis* teeth was characteristic of our lineage. *Orrorin tugenensis* found in Kenya and dated at just less than 6 million years old has ape-like teeth and forelimbs, but bones from the thigh suggest that it was adapted for bipedality. Slightly younger are a collection of fossils from Ethiopia known as *Ardipithecus* dated at 5.8 to 4.4 mya. In 2009 a detailed scientific analysis was published of the fossil *Ardipithecus ramidus*, known as Ardi, that was found 15 years earlier. She is the youngest of the group dated at 4.4 million years and has received a lot of attention because the fossil is relatively complete and consists of a mosaic of both ape-like and human-like features. In all hominids a small bone in the foot articulates in such a way that the big toe lines up with the rest of the toes and provides a strong "toe off" that is critical to efficient bipedalism. In the apes it is oriented differently allowing for the big toe to be used for grasping tree limbs. Ardi's foot resembled an ape in this respect, but the rest of her foot had characteristics that would allow her to walk upright. As a result of this *Ardipithecus* is thought to have been quadruped in the trees, but bipedal on the ground.

Walking upright has been a crucial characteristic of the hominid lineage. Ardi's mosaic of features has some people wanting to classify her as an australopithecine. A small bone in her foot that has been retained in the hominid line from ancient apes and monkeys, kept the foot more rigid for upright walking. Her upper pelvis is short and broad with other features that further enhance a bipedal stride and are rarely seen except in other hominids. However, her lower pelvis is completely ape-like. Most interesting is her hand. Modern African apes have hands adapted for climbing, but they also support their weight on their knuckles when walking on the ground. The prevailing view has been that knuckle walking is the primitive condition that our ancestors went through on their way to walking upright. However, Ardi's hand looks like she walked and climbed in trees more like a monkey than any living African ape. This then suggests that our ancestors might never have passed through the chimp-like knuckle-walking stage on our way to becoming human. Otherwise it would mean that our ancestors would have very early on evolved chimp-like adaptations, lost them, and then reverted to the primitive condition by the time Ardi had evolved. Ardi's discoverers think this is unlikely. Yet others argue all kinds of apes were running around in the Miocene between 5 and 23 mya. While Ardi clearly had the beginnings of many human-like traits, whether she evolved into an australopithecine is not known. She might have instead been one of evolution's many experiments that went extinct.

AUSTRALOPITHECINES

Australopithecines are the oldest group that clearly walked upright and are unequivocally in the hominid line and lived from about 4.4 mya to 2.0 mya. They had a brain size that was equal to or slightly larger than that of the chimp ranging from approximately 400 cubic centimetres (cc) (the average size for chimps) to 500 cc. Fossil remains have been found all over Africa occupying a wide variety of different niches. They still retain several ape-like features including long arms. They had large teeth for chewing, but also showed a thickening of tooth enamel characteristic of all later hominids. The oldest member of this group is *Australopithecus anamensis* dated 4.2 to 3.9 mya. *Australopithecus afarensis* includes the famous Lucy (so named because when she was discovered "Lucy in the Sky with Diamonds" was playing in the camp). These fossils were found in Eastern Africa and date from 3.9 to 3.0 mya. *Australopithecus afarensis* had short legs in relationship to their hands and arms and chest, suggesting that they still spent a lot of time in the trees. However, footsteps found in Laetoli dated at 3. 6 million years confirm that Lucy was fully upright. *Australopithecus africanus* fossils have been discovered exclusively in southern Africa and are from 3.0 to 2.5 million years old. *Australopithecus garhi* was contemporaneous with *A. afarensis* and had front teeth like a hominid, but still had enormous cheek teeth. Three species, *Australopithecus aethiopcius* (2.6–2.3 mya) *Australopithecus robustus* (2.1–1.5 mya), and *Australopithecus boisei* (2.1–1.1 mya) are known as robust australopithecines. The cranium is more heavily built due to dietary specialization and they have never been in serious contention as direct ancestors of *Homo*. Many paleoanthropologists now classify them in the genus *Paranthropus,* another bipedal ape.

It may not ever be possible to know which australopithecine evolved into *Homo*, but various trends continued. Brain capacity increased dramatically and steadily. A continuation in the reduction of teeth and jaw occurred. *Homo* co-existed with australopithecines in Africa for more than a million years, beginning approximately 2.5 mya. *Homo habilis* (2.3–1.6 mya) is called handy man because it is with this fossil that we find the first evidence of stone tools. Its body is still much like australopithecine. Brain capacity ranges from 500 to 800 cc, overlapping with australopithecine at the low end and *H. erectus* at the high end. A brain cast of one skull shows a slight bulge in an area that indicates *H. habilis* might have been capable of rudimentary speech. It has been a controversial species because some authorities think the variation between the different specimens is too great to be considered just one species. *H. habilis* illustrates a basic debate that exists over the naming of hominid fossils. There are the "lumpers" who want fewer species and the "splitters" who almost every time a new fossil is discovered claim it is a new species. Regardless, of how individual fossils are classified, it is apparent that the human family tree had many branches and most of them went extinct.

HOMO

Homo erectus was our first ancestor to leave Africa and has been found in Asia and Europe. It existed from 1.8 mya to 300,000 years ago, overlapping with both australopithecines and archaic *H. sapiens* (also known as *Homo heidelbergensis*). Once again a dramatic increase in brain size occurred. Much more sophisticated tools have been found and it is thought that *H. erectus* used fire. The oldest specimens are more robust in their build while the more recent ones are thinner boned. Archaic *H. sapiens* first appeared 600,000 years ago and are found as recently as 200,000 years ago. They refer to a group of skulls that have characteristics of both *H. erectus* and modern humans and it is quite difficult to classify many of these fossils as belonging to either one group or the other. In 2003 *Homo floresiensis* was discovered on the Indonesian island of Flores. Nicknamed the hobbit, it was only about a meter tall and had an astonishingly small brain size of 380 cc. Several more *H. floresiensis* fossils have been found and dated between 38,000 and 12,000 years old. How to classify this fossil has also been difficult. Stone tools dated at 840,000 years have been found and many researchers thought the Hobbit was a dwarf form of *H. erectus*. Dwarfing is often observed on islands as a result of a limited food supply, few predators, and few species competing for the same environmental niche. Survival would depend on minimizing daily energy requirements. However, no fossils of large-bodied ancestors have ever been found and its recent age suggests that *H. floresiensis* either arrived on the island in its petite form or descended from an early dispersal of archaic *Homo* that had undergone dwarfism. The small brain size is as small as any australopithecine ever discovered, and fairly typical for a chimpanzee. Various hypotheses were suggested to explain the hobbit's small brain, including microcephaly, Laron syndrome and endemic cretinism. None of them have any significant following any more. Where the hobbit fits into the human family tree is a story that is still evolving. But this species certainly brings into question the importance of brain size. How big a brain do you need to make tools? Unfortunately brain size alone gives no information about the actual organization of the brain. One of the unsolved mysteries in human evolution is our big brain. In about a million years the cranial capacity doubled as Australopithecines evolved into *H. erectus*. It then doubled again in another million years with the emergence of *H. sapiens*. In evolutionary terms this is a mere blink. What kind of selection pressure could have brought about this extraordinarily rapid change? See Figure 5.2 for a time line of the Hominidae.

Figure 5.2 Timeline for Hominidae

Sahelanthropus tchadensis*	6 to 7 million years BCE
Orrorin tugenensi*	5.9 to 6 million years BCE
Ardipithecus ramidus**	5.8 to 4.4 million years BCE
Australopithecus anamenis	4.2 to 3.9 million years BCE
Australopithecus afarensis	3.9 to 3.0 million years BCE
Australopithecus garhi	3.9 to 3.0 million years BCE
Australopithecus africanus	3.0 to 2.5 million years BCE
Australopithecus aethiopcius[+]	2.6 to 2.3 million years BCE
Australopithecus robustus[+]	2.1 to 1.5 million years BCE
Australopithecus boise[+]	2.1 to 1.1 million years BCE
Homo habilis	2.3 to 1.6 million years BCE
Homo erectus	1.8 to 0.3 million years BCE
Homo sapiens	400,000 to 200,000 years BCE
Homo sapiens neandertalensis	230,000 to 30,000 years BCE
Homo floresiensis	38,000 to 12,000 years BCE
Homo sapiens sapiens	130,000 years BCE to present

* There is still some controversy as to whether these species should be classified as hominids
** Some paleoanthropologists think this fossil should be classified as an Australopithecus
[+]These species are known as robust australopithecines and many paleo-anthropologists now classify them in the genus *Paranthropus*

NEANDERTHALS

Neanderthals existed between 230,000 and 28,000 years ago and have been found throughout Eurasia. The classification of this species also has been controversial. The term archaic *H. sapiens* refers to an early form or subspecies, but anatomically distinct from the modern form. Not all archaic populations necessarily evolved into anatomically modern humans. The European Neanderthals were considered an archaic form, but at different times they have been considered a subspecies of *H. sapiens,* the ancestor that evolved into *H. sapiens,* or essentially us. Their brain capacity was bigger than anatomically modern humans, but relative to their body size was not. Although on average they were shorter, they were powerfully built with thick heavy bones, barreled chested and adapted for cold harsh climates. Those found in Europe are considered classic Neanderthals. Those found in the Middle East were more finely boned. Excellent hunters, they had many more tools and weapons that were far more advanced than those associated with *H. erectus*. They were the first people known to have buried their dead. DNA has been successfully extracted from several different Neanderthal fossils. The lack of diversity in Neanderthal mitochondrial DNA (mtDNA) sequences, combined with the large differences between Neanderthal and modern human mtDNA, suggests that Neanderthal diverged from the modern human lineage more than 500,000 years ago. In 2010 from a variety of different fossil bones Svante Paabo and his team reported that they had sequenced about 60 percent of the Neanderthal genome. Comparing this sequence with sequences of modern populations (see below), it is now thought that Neanderthal may have interbred with anatomically modern humans with whom they coexisted for thousands of years. It is estimated that any human whose ancestral group developed out of Africa (Neanderthal has not been found in Africa) has between 1 and 4 percent Neanderthal DNA in them. It is important to realize that these claims are based on a statistical analysis of various fragments. Although more and more DNA is being extracted from Neanderthal fossils, it is not a complete sequence. In addition a great deal of variety exists at particular loci within present-day human populations. Genetic sequencing data is a very powerful kind of information, but it also needs to be combined with other kinds of information.

Anatomically modern humans have been found dated at 195,000 years ago and have an average brain size of about 1,350 cc. With the appearance of anatomically modern man in Europe, 40,000 years ago, a dramatic change in the type of cultural artifacts occurred. Decorated tools, beads, ivory carvings of humans and animals, clay figurines, musical instruments, and spectacular cave paintings appeared over the next 20,000 years. Thus the prevailing view was that modern humans were simply a lot smarter than Neanderthals and out competed them, driving them to extinction. Nevertheless, we now have evidence that Neanderthals engaged in many practices that were thought to be unique to modern humans. They also carry the same *FOXP2* gene that is thought to be associated with language. This gene differs at two different points from the gene in chimpanzees and it has been postulated that this is one of the reasons humans can speak, but chimps cannot.

In recent years the role of climate has been receiving increasing attention as a significant factor in Neanderthal's disappearance.

Approximately 55,000 years ago the climate in Eurasia began to fluctuate wildly from very frigid to more mild and back in just a matter of decades. Previously, the changes had been much slower allowing Neanderthals to adapt, but possibly they were unable to adjust to such rapid changes and by 30,000 years ago only a few isolated populations survived on the Iberian Peninsula with its relatively mild climate and rich resources. But as with any species, if numbers become too small they are unable to sustain themselves and inbreeding can become a serious problem. Furthermore, under the pressure of rapid climate change, subtle differences in behavior between the two species may have been enough to doom the Neanderthal to extinction. Several ideas have been put forth. Needles left by moderns suggest that they sewed their clothes and tents and that might have provided better protection against the cold. Perhaps modern humans were much less picky in what they ate. Neanderthals were heavily dependent on large mammals, which became increasingly rare with climate change while moderns supplemented their diets with all kinds of plant material. A more varied diet would have favored a division of labor, men specializing in the hunt of large game while women and children gathered seeds, nuts and berries. Eating meat has long been considered to be a crucial factor in the evolution of large brains, but even in modern-day hunting and gathering societies the bulk of calories is supplied by gathering. The division of labor would have provided a more stable food supply and safer environment for raising children. A variety of different kinds of research suggest that the energy requirements for Neanderthals were considerably higher than for modern humans. In times of environmental stress and food scarcity this could be the difference between survival and death. Even in times of plenty modern humans were more fuel efficient, freeing up calories for reproduction and raising young. Around 30,000 years ago the numbers of modern humans who lived to become grandparents showed a dramatic increase for unknown reasons. This would have two important consequences. First, it lengthened the reproductive years, increasing fertility potential. It also made possible a longer time to acquire specialized knowledge such as where to find drinking water in times of drought and to teach it to the next generation. Learning has been the hallmark of our species and has allowed us to spread around the globe unlike any previous species.

Undoubtedly a combination of factors contributed to the extinction of Neanderthals. While modern humans might have been responsible for the demise or absorption of some populations of Neanderthals, this was not true of all of them. The last remaining population lived in the caves of Gibraltar 28,000 years ago. We have no evidence of modern humans settling there until thousands of years later.

OUT-OF-AFRICA: THE MOLECULAR EVIDENCE

Molecular evidence has revolutionized the study of human origins, but as is often the case with new findings that contradict the received view, it was initially greeted with skepticism. In 1967 Allan Wilson and Vincent Sarich called for a major revision of the human family tree. Based on immunological comparison of serum albumins they suggested the common ancestor of humans, chimpanzees, and gorillas lived only about 5 mya. This was significantly more recent than the 15 million years or more advocated by paleoanthropologists based on fossil evidence. As more fossils were found and the techniques of Sarich and Wilson became more refined, consensus emerged that the human–ape split occurred between 5 and 8 mya. Geneticist Luigi Luc Cavalli-Sforza had begun a new area of research by combining concrete findings from demography with a newly available analysis of blood groups in human populations to investigate the origin and diversity of human populations. Building on the work of Cavalli-Sforza, in 1987 Wilson with co-workers Rebecca Cann and Mark Stoneking announced that they had evidence that the most recent maternal ancestor of all living humans was a woman living in Africa about 200,000 years ago. Based on analysis of mtDNA taken from 147 individuals representing different races and geographic origins, this became known as the "Eve hypothesis," "Garden of Eden hypothesis," or the "Out-of-Africa hypothesis." Once again this finding caused considerable controversy as well as a lot of misunderstanding of what mitochondrial Eve represents. The techniques of DNA sequencing and DNA-relatedness comparisons have improved dramatically since 1987. The Out-of-Africa hypothesis has been confirmed with a much larger database, suggesting an origin of about 170,000 years. In the late 1990s analysis of markers on the Y chromosome suggests an even more recent origin of about 50,000 years. This data supports what is known as the replacement model. Archaic forms of *H. sapiens* evolved in Europe, Asia and Africa, but they were all replaced by anatomically modern humans who evolved from a small population in Africa about 200,000 years ago, leaving Africa between 55,000 and 60,000 years ago. In this view *H. erectus* and Neanderthals made no contribution to the modern genotype. These dates will undoubtedly continue to be revised as more data is analyzed and the analytical techniques continue to improve. Ironically, genetic data that appeared to have disproved the competing **multiregional hypothesis** is now getting new life with the most recent data suggesting that Neanderthals and modern humans interbred.

The multiregional hypothesis proposed by Milford Wolpoff in the 1980s posited that modern humans evolved simultaneously from *H. erectus* in all parts of the world. Many archeologists and paleoanthropologists favored this model, claiming that the fossils exhibited regional continuity with racial characteristics becoming established very early on. *H. erectus* found in China looked more like modern-day Chinese than like African *H. erectus* and modern Africans looked more like the fossils found in Africa. Nevertheless, in terms of other organisms' history, it virtually never happens that several distinct populations all evolve into one species and Wolpoff always had an uphill battle. This theory continued to lose ground as the molecular evidence against it appeared to be quite compelling. Modern African populations show the most genetic diversity, suggesting that they are the oldest populations. The oldest anatomically modern fossils have also been found in Africa. Today we have genetic evidence that some of the dramatic differences between races such as skin pigmentation, hair color and texture, and body form are quite recent adaptations that arose in small isolated populations responding to local conditions. The amount of skin pigmentation correlates to the amount of solar radiation. Dark skin protects against tissue and metabolic damage and is common in peoples found near the equator. However, people found in the higher latitudes tend to lose pigmentation because although ultraviolet radiation in high amounts is damaging it also catalyzes the synthesis of vitamin D in the skin. Based on DNA extracted from Neanderthal fossils, some scientists have suggested that Neanderthal might have been a redhead with fair skin. Body shape varies geographically in a way that correlates with changes in temperature. Being round and short conserves heat and is found in people in the northern regions and high altitudes. Having long limbs allows for more efficient dissipation of heat and is characteristic of peoples originating in the tropics.

Proponents of regional continuity point out problems with molecular dating techniques and the limited amount of data. The study of ancient DNA is still a relatively young field that has several methodological problems associated with it. This includes small sample sizes, problematic methods of group definition, and and the need to modify the analytical methods that were initially developed for modern samples. The most serious problem is that of contamination, which includes DNA from archeologists at the excavation site and from all the various researchers in the subsequent handling of the fossil. Non-human DNA is also another source, particularly at the site. Wilson, who also provided the first reliable genetic data of the mammoth, began his presentation with, "We have learned today that the mammoth was either an elephant or fungus." As exciting as this technique is, it is only one tool for the study of human evolution and in many cases other sources of information may be more appropriate. In the Levant (a site in Syria) stone tools show continuity between those from the Middle Paleolithic made by Neanderthals, and the Upper Paleolithic made by modern humans. Furthermore, the latest sequence data suggests that Neanderthals and modern humans *did* interbreed. Many researchers now advocate a somewhat modified multiregional hypothesis. In the assimilation model, humans arose in Africa, but a certain amount of gene flow between Africa, Asia and Europe occurred allowing local populations to evolve together and preventing reproductive isolation. Assimilation and selection rather than complete replacement contributed to the modern genotype in populations outside of Africa. Replacement with hybridization incorporates the most recent genetic data that suggests that only 90 percent of non-nuclear DNA from populations outside of Africa has African roots and supports the view that archaic forms of *Homo* have contributed to the modern genotype. Nevertheless, most researchers still think that the majority of modern human characteristics evolved in Africa between 200,000 and 150,000 years ago, but only spread out of Africa about 50,000 years ago. Yet both genetic data and recent fossil finds suggest that the migration patterns of our ancestors were much more complex than previously thought. The interaction between anatomically modern and archaic populations remains a topic of intense debate.

THE GENOGRAPHIC PROJECT

Much of what we know about the migration patterns of our ancestors is based on data from the Genographic Project, which is collecting DNA samples from indigenous and traditional peoples along with the general public all over the world to continue the analysis that Cavalli-Sforza began. Molecular evidence is also providing insight into the origins of a vast array of cultural practices from when humans first began wearing clothes to how various religious, economical and other social institutions evolved. However, it is important not to over-interpret the evidence. DNA is an important source of data, but it does not stand alone and must be used in conjunction with other information. Cultural anthropologists have shown that kinship systems in many societies do not necessarily correspond to biological relatedness. Thus, mtDNA analysis of people buried together may show they are biologically related, but it cannot be taken as evidence of matrilineal relationships.

The Genographic Project has already greatly enriched our understanding of the early history of *H. sapiens*. It has shown that the humans are still evolving. This has important ramifications for our understanding of disease, which will be discussed in the next chapter. However, a variety of scientific, legal and ethical problems have been associated with genetic research. The Human Genome Diversity Project (HGDP) as initially proposed by Cavalli-Sforza and his colleagues did not go forward, because of a rash of criticism that reflected recognition of the rights of indigenous peoples and concern of how this research could be used. A prevailing attitude of the West has been that scientific study trumps all other concerns, but such research does not occur in a vacuum. Studies on human genetic variation have many implications, including possible social, economic, medical, and legal discrimination against particular groups. It could also be used to perpetuate a racist ideology. Ironically, the genome project and blood sampling has shown that the concept of race has no biological foundation, and is literally only skin deep. Far more genetic variation exists within racial groups than between them, but that still does not prevent people from misusing the data. The genetic data may also contradict the oral history and deeply held religious beliefs about a group's origins. The physical act of sampling may be morally and/or spiritually repugnant to some groups. Data continues to be collected, but with more attention being paid (and some say still not enough) to these kinds of issues. DNA has now been recovered from various fossil remains, but the use of ancient DNA also has its own set of problems. In 1996 the nearly complete skeletal remains of an individual that became known as Kennewick man were found near the banks of the Columbia River in Washington State. A controversy emerged in which the scientific study of the remains was in conflict with the rights of descendants of ancient peoples. In a legal battle that lasted almost eight years eight anthropologists successfully sued for the right to study the bones after the United States government seized them on behalf of Native American tribal groups who claimed Kennewick man as an ancestor and wanted to rebury his skeleton. Genes are being used to tell new stories, but what are those stories saying about others and us, science and society, and the intersection of nature and culture? Genetic research holds the possibility of explaining historical events that were previously inaccessible and can be used to contest oppression and racism. But just like the evolutionary stories that are being told, genetic stories also evolve and are embedded in the culture, time, and place from which they emerge. Thus new research proposals should be evaluated not just in terms of their scientific merit, but should also address the social, political and legal implications of such research.

FURTHER READING

Cartmill, M., Pilbeam, D., Isaac, G. (1986) "One hundred years of paleo-anthropology," *American Scientist* 74(4): 410–20.

Darwin, C. ([1871] 1981) *The Descent of Man*, Princeton: Princeton University Press.

——([1872] 1965) *The Expression of the Emotions in Man and Animals,* Chicago: University of Chicago Press.

Gould, S. (1982) "Piltown revisted," in *The Panda's Thumb,* New York: W. W. Norton & Co.

Huxley, T. ([1863] 1898) *Man's Place in Nature*, vol. 7 of *Collected Essays*, New York: D. Appleton & Co.

McHenry, H. (2009) "Human evolution," in M. Ruse and J. Travis (eds) *Evolution: The First Four Billion Years,* Cambridge, MA: Belknap Press.

Wade, N. (2007) *Before the Dawn: Recovering the Lost History of Our Ancestors*, New York: Penguin.

WEBSITES

Becoming Human bib.becominghuman.org/

The TalkOrigins Archives bib.talkorigins.org/

The Genographic Project https://genographic.nationalgeographic.com/genographic/index.html

Tracing Ancestry with mtDNA bib.pbs.org/wgbh/nova/neanderthals/mtdna.html

6

ORIGINS, THE EXPANSION OF LIFE, AND THE PERSISTENCE OF DISEASE

LIFE'S BEGINNINGS

Although Darwin titled his book *On the Origin of Species*, it was not really about the origin of species, but rather how species descended from other species. It provided little insight into how life first emerged, the evolution of cellular organization, or how the genetic code developed. To be fair it was not possible to even investigate such questions in a meaningful way until relatively recently. Darwin did speculate how life might have begun. In an oft-quoted letter to his good friend Joseph Hooker, he imagined a warm little pond with a variety of ammonia and phosphoric salts. Energy from heat, light, and electricity could lead to the formation of proteins and over time more complex changes would occur leading to simple life forms. Darwin recognized that such a process could not occur today, because living creatures would instantly devour any molecules, eliminating any possibility to evolve into anything more complex. Darwin's speculations drew on some key ideas that were well established by the nineteenth century, the most important being that the basis of life was the molecular processes occurring within the cell. Proteins were recognized as crucial to many biological processes. Although nucleic acids had been identified, it would be many years before their importance would be understood. Chemists had independently synthesized in the laboratory urea, alanine, and sugars from inorganic compounds and had demonstrated that the gap between living and non-living was not insurmountable.

Huxley brought these findings to the general public. Appearing before an Edinburgh audience with nothing more than a bottle of smelling salts, water, and various other common substances, he claimed that he had all the basic ingredients of protoplasm or what he translated as the physical basis of life. All organisms shared a unity of form, they shared a similar chemical composition and, although differences between plants and animals appeared to be very different, no sharp dividing line existed between the simplest of these organisms. The difference between living and non-living matter lay in the arrangement of the molecules. He maintained that even thoughts "are the expression of molecular changes in the matter of life which is the source of our other vital phenomena." Nevertheless, how life emerged from non-life was still mysterious and theories abounded. The nineteenth century also saw a contentious debate over spontaneous generation in which Huxley and Michael Faraday played a prominent role. It was not until the 1920s that speculation over life's origins began to be turned into testable hypotheses. A. I. Oparin (1894–1980), J. B. S. Haldane (1892–1964) and others proposed that the abiotic (without the use of biologic agents) synthesis of organic compounds formed a primordial soup, much like the pond that Darwin had envisioned. The soup became increasingly rich and from this the first life forms eventually arose. However, the two men differed as to how and what those first forms were like. Haldane thought that viruses arose prior to cells while Oparin thought that colloidal gel-like systems formed that eventually gave rise to anaerobic creatures that could absorb organic compounds directly from the environment, using them for growth and reproduction. These two ideas provided a basic conceptual framework that has guided subsequent research and also highlight a fundamental question that underlies all origin of life research. How does one define life? The two different hypotheses are indicative of two basic characteristics of living organisms, metabolism and replication (as distinct from reproduction). Both are necessary for life as we know it. Something could grow and divide, but without a genetic replicating mechanism, something as complex as a cell could not evolve. Did both of these capabilities arise together, or in a sequence and if so what came first? Before attempting to answer this question, another question must also be addressed. What were the conditions in which life first emerged?

For a long time it was thought that the origin and early evolution of life took several billion years. However, evidence of life continues to be pushed back to earlier and earlier times. The 3.5-billion-year-old Australia Warrawoona formation contains microstructures that were thought to have a biological origin. Known as **stromatolites**, these are laminated rocks that are usually formed by the action of blue-green algae. However, sometimes they are the result of abiotic processes. Many people have disputed the origin of the stromatolites in the Warrawoona formation, but other kinds of analyses of the same site as well as analyses of a 3.4-billion-year-old site in South Africa provide convincing evidence that over 3 billion years ago the earth was already swarming with **prokaryotes**. Rather than life being extremely unlikely, it appears that as soon as conditions were suitable for life, life appeared. A crucial factor may have been liquid water − as soon as the earth's surface cooled to below the boiling point of water, life quickly emerged. However, we have no direct evidence geological or otherwise of what the earth's early environment was like in terms of the ocean pH, the components of the atmosphere, the temperature, and a variety of other conditions that may have been critical for life to develop. Several different scenarios have been proposed.

In 1953 Stanley Miller (1930–2007) and Harold Urey (1893–1981) published the results of their classic primordial soup experiment based on what they thought the earth's early atmosphere was like. A series of sterile sealed flasks and tubes containing water (H_2O), ammonia (NH_3), methane (CH_4) and hydrogen (H_2) were connected in a loop. One flask was half full of water and another had a pair of electrodes. The water was heated to boiling to induce evaporation. Sparks between the electrodes simulated lightening through the atmosphere and the water vapor. The atmosphere was allowed to cool causing the water to condense and drip back into the first flask, and the cycle was repeated. After a week the results were analyzed. Amino acids and simple sugars were formed, and later experiments showed that **purines** and **pyrimidines**, the building blocks for RNA and DNA, were also formed. However, current models no longer think that the early earth's atmosphere was as Miller and Urey proposed. The reducing gases that were critical, CH_4 and NH_3 are now thought to have been rare and found only near volcanoes or hydrothermal vents. Instead, most models today assume that the earth's early atmosphere was neutral or weakly reducing, consisting of a mixture of carbon dioxide (CO_2), nitrogen (N_2), carbon monoxide (CO) and water (H_2O), along with lesser amounts of hyposulphurous acid (H_2SO_2) and hydrogen sulfide (H_2S). In lieu of these findings and other kinds of evidence, several alternatives and modifications to the primordial soup have been suggested.

The discovery of deep-ocean hydrothermal vents teaming with life astonished scientists. No sunlight, enormous pressures, toxic chemicals, extremes of heat and cold; it is hard to imagine a harsher environment for living organisms. Yet life has thrived for millions of years in these conditions. Rather than using energy from the sun, energy is obtained by oxidizing H_2S. The hydrogen-rich fluids and high temperatures around the vent are conducive to the synthesis of organic compounds, which suggested to some researchers that this is where life first formed. Various minerals that are found in vent environments may have also played a critical role. Not only can they catalyze and speed up chemical reactions, they can also help stabilize organic molecules once formed, preventing them from breaking down. In addition, deep in the sea organisms would have been protected from the harsh conditions caused by large-impact events that were thought to be quite frequent in earth's early history. Organisms would have been relatively unaffected by the periodic mass-extinction events that devastated those living on or near the surface. Finally, not only do the micro-organisms appear to be some of the oldest known organisms, the animals in the vents appear to be more closely related to ancient animals than anything else today. For all of these reasons, it is plausible that this was where life first formed.

Most origin research has assumed that life arose in some variant of Darwin's warm pond. Some researchers, most notably Miller, his former student Jeffrey Bada, and Lelie Orgel have argued that life began in ice, at temperatures that few organisms can survive today. In 1972 Miller filled vials with ammonia and cyanide, molecules that were thought to be common in the earth's early atmosphere. He sealed the vials and cooled them down to $-108°$ F, the temperature of Jupiter's icy moon Europa. For 25 years he kept the vials in their icy state and in 1997 he analyzed the contents and found that both nucleobases and amino acids had formed. Although life requires liquid water, microscopic pockets of liquid can exist in ice crystals at temperature as low as -60° F. The ice could concentrate simple molecules, assembling them into longer chains. A cubic yard of sea ice can contain more than a million liquid compartments – a million tiny test tubes of different chemical cocktails – and perhaps one of those cocktails was the right mix for life. Bada argues that cold is actually much more conducive to the chemistry of life. In general most chemical reactions slow down as the temperature drops and according to standard calculations nothing should have formed in Miller's icy vials even if he had run the experiment for another hundred years. However, strange things happen when chemicals are frozen in ice and some reactions are actually speeded up. In a process called eutectic freezing, as an ice crystal grows it remains pure, adding only water and forcing out molecules such as salt or cyanide into the liquid compartments, concentrating them and causing them to collide more often. Freezing not only concentrates molecules, but it also helps preserve fragile molecules such as nucelobases and this would allow them to assemble into larger chains, interact and perhaps eventually give rise to something more interesting. Furthermore, according to some models of solar evolution, the sun was about 30 percent dimmer than today. After the rain of asteroids stopped, some scientists think the earth was essentially one giant snowball, the oceans having a crust of ice as much as 1 thousand feet thick. Eutectic freezing appears to do more than just concentrate molecules. Hauke Trinks found that the surface of the ice is a mixture of positive and negative charges and there also exists a strong bonding between the surface of the ice and the liquid. These bonds are important for the assembly of long molecules. Trinks hypothesizes that the charges could grab the nucelobases, stacking them up and eventually forming an RNA molecule.

Other researchers have proposed that life on earth was seeded from an extraterrestrial impact, either a meteorite or from comets. Findings from NASA have identified various building blocks of life found in outer space, and amino acids and other organics have been found in meteorites that are 4.5 billion years old. Even if life has an extraterrestrial origin, it does not answer the question of how life actually arose, but changes the location to outer space or another planet. Regardless of which theory turns out to be correct, whether life came from outer space, arose in a deep sea vent, or in a frozen ocean, or some combination, all of these scenarios suggest that simple life forms might be relatively common in the universe. Under a variety of different conditions the building blocks of life will form. The primordial soup undoubtedly had ingredients from many different sources: abiotic syntheses in a reducing atmosphere, metal-sulfide-mediated syntheses from deep-sea vents, and organics arriving via meteorites, comets, and interplanetary dust. However, it is still not well understood how these monomers of simple sugars, amino acids and nucleotide bases were assembled into long chains. This is one of the two major unsolved problems in origin-of-life research. Long-chained, complicated, organic molecules also do not constitute life. The second major problem is the transition to something that contains a genetic replication system based on nucleic acid. Many biologists think the precursor to the DNA-based world of life was an intermediary **RNA world**.

THE RNA WORLD

When the role of DNA was first worked out it was often referred to as a self-replicating molecule, but this is not true. It needs RNA and a host of enzymes to carry out its job. Even the simplest organisms have a very complicated apparatus of membranes, enzymes, ribosomes, and different kinds of RNA that make possible DNA replication. The first forms of life were probably not DNA based or a virus as Haldane envisioned, as viruses need the machinery of the cell to reproduce. While proteins are highly versatile molecules and involved in virtually all aspects of cell metabolism as enzymes, as well as providing much of the structure of the cell, they don't seem to have the ability to carry information from generation to generation; RNA, however, has the ability to carry out both functions. Like DNA it can carry information in its code, but it also has some enzymatic capabilities. One of the important tasks that enzymes do is cut out useless sequences from RNA after it has been transcribed from DNA; RNA can loop back on its self and edit itself, cutting out particular sequences. By selecting for particular variants in the lab, researchers have shown that RNA can evolve. In the right environment, RNA can act like an enzyme slicing DNA and other molecules. It can bind to atoms and cells and join molecules together, even amino acids. In short, RNA can perform many of the functions that are necessary to a cell that are now performed by DNA and proteins. Different forms of RNA might have evolved, eventually hooking amino acids together to create proteins that in turn helped RNA replicate faster. Eventually RNA might have made a double-stranded related molecule: DNA. DNA still had the ability to mutate, crucial for further evolution, yet would have been more stable and more reliable for storing information. This would have led to greater efficiency. Eventually DNA and proteins took over many of RNA's tasks and life as we know it began, continuing to evolve. While major gaps remain in our understanding of the transition from the abiotic synthesis of organic compounds to the evolution of something as complex as a cell, molecular sequencing data has revolutionized our understanding of how life evolved from that first cell.

RETHINKING THE TREE OF LIFE: MICROBIAL EVOLUTION

Microbes receive short shrift in most treatments of evolution as well as general biology books. Yet micro-organisms are what make all life possible. They constitute the bulk of the cellular biomass of the planet and it is their interactions that define and support the biosphere. If animals and plants were to disappear life would still continue, but the same could not be said if microbes disappeared. They are the main players in our vast global ecosystem. Until relatively recently the living world was divided into two fundamental groups: eukaryotes (animals, plants, fungi, and protists) and prokaryotes or bacteria. The defining characteristic of eukaryotes was the possession of a distinct membrane-bound nucleus. If an organism lacked a nucleus it was classified as a prokaryote. Prokaryotes were thus defined negatively, by the absence of certain traits. Such a classification is heavily biased in favor of only the last billion years of evolution when multi-celled plants and animals first evolved. Prokaryotes have been around since life first appeared, representing over 3 billion years of evolution. Bacteria invented photosynthesis, the defining characteristic of plants and aerobic respiration that allowed animals to breathe. Yet we remained largely ignorant of their vast diversity and classification of them has been highly problematic. For Carl Woese bacterial phylogenies are not just filling in the missing pieces of the Darwinian program. Bacterial evolution is itself the puzzle. It holds the key to the origin of life, to the origin of the eukaryotic cell, and to an historical account of life on this planet. Once the tools of molecular biology became available in the late 1950s and 1960s researchers recognized that the linear sequences of amino acids in proteins and the base sequences of nucleic acids were a kind of molecular fossil record documenting the organismal evolutionary history, extending investigations into the history of life by some 3 billion years. Such sequences were just as informative and complex in prokaryotes as in eukaryotes.

Previous classification of bacteria had been hampered by several factors. They had far fewer morphological characteristics than multi-celled organisms or even a single-celled eukaryote, and it was also extremely difficult to decide which cellular features and characteristics would be the most useful for taxonomic purposes. Furthermore, one major aspect of the species concept did not apply: the inability to reproduce with members of another species since bacteria reproduce asexually. Molecular sequence data held out the promise to be able to classify bacteria phylogenetically, i.e. to tell who descended from whom. Finally it would be possible to root a universal tree of life. However, bacteria from different taxa engage in extensive **lateral gene transfer** (LGT), meaning they swap genes with each other. This meant that tracing the genealogy of a gene did not necessarily reflect the history of the organism. Depending on what sequence or gene was picked, a variety of different phylogenetic trees could be built. The molecular data initially caused more problems than it solved and various schemes were proposed.

The RNA of ribosomes (or rRNA) was decided to be the sequence data of choice for determining the genealogical relationships of bacteria. Ribosomes were picked because they are found in all species and these genes were regarded as central to biological function, critical to turning the information contained in the DNA into a functioning protein. Ribosomal sequence data contradicted many of the existing major bacterial classification schemes. Furthermore, rather than a simple bifurcation between eukaryotes and prokaryotes, a third major group emerged, initially called archaebacteria. In gross morphology they resembled bacteria, but detailed molecular sequence data showed they were no more closely related to other prokaryotes than to eukaryotes. They were found in unusual environments that at first glance seemed unsuitable for life, which suggested that they were very old, perhaps the first organisms on the newly habitable, but still not very hospitable planet earth. They existed in anaerobic environments such as hot springs and sulfur springs, in brine, and were even found growing in smoldering coal refuse piles. Rather than a group of unrelated organisms that had special adaptations to their extreme environments, grouping them together suggested they had conserved common characteristics from a very ancient lineage.

The archaebacteria shared a variety of core traits that were unique and quite different from other bacteria. These included a different chemical structure of their lipid cell membrane, a cell wall lacking peptidoglycan (also known as murein), which had been considered a defining feature of prokaryotes. Most important they had unique enzymes responsible for transcribing DNA to RNA. As more and more organisms were examined it indicated that the archaebacteria were actually more closely related to eukaryotes than to bacteria. As a result of this, in 1990 Woese who had been a leader in this research proposed there should be three kingdoms. **Archaea** (archaebacteria), Bacteria (eubacteria), and Eukarya (eukaryotes). The universal ancestor gave rise to two branches, Bacteria on one and Archaea and Eukaryotes on the other. A major controversy surrounded this suggestion with many prominent biologists still wanting to maintain the eukaryotic/prokaryotic distinction. They claimed that no amount of variation in sequence data between Archaea and Bacteria could compare to the complexity of organization of the eukaryotic cell, which was what made possible the development and evolution of the diverse forms of life we see today. Sequence data can be considered morphological data as well, albeit at a different level of analysis. Why should it be privileged over all other kinds of data? Various schemes were suggested. Based on heat shock proteins and other morphological characteristics it was proposed that the eukaryotic cell arose from the fusion of an archaebacteria and a gram-negative bacterium. Other kinds of data also disputed that archaebacteria clustered with the eukaryotes. In spite of continual controversy archaebacteria were considered sufficiently different from other bacteria and the three-domain system prevailed (see **Figure 6.1**).

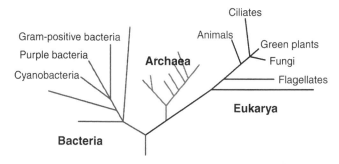

Figure 6.1 The three domains

From the 1970s through the mid-1990s the relationship of the three groups to each other remained problematic. Were Archaea the oldest of the three different groups or did they diverge more recently from bacteria? Where did eukaryotes come from? Were eukaroytes relatively modern or did they arise shortly after life arose, perhaps evolving from Archaea? Were they a product of several fusion events engulfing a variety of different bacteria? Perhaps they represented a fundamental third group with a lineage of descent distinct from both archaea and bacteria. In the 1990s further research was able to answer some of these questions and surprised everyone. The symbiotic origin of chloroplasts and mitochondria, which had been postulated for many years, was confirmed, indicating that they had once been free-living bacteria and were then engulfed by another organism. The biggest surprise was what was discovered about the eukaryotic nuclear genome. It was a molecular chimera consisting of genes from all three domains. Some informational/translation genes came from archaea while some metabolic genes came from bacteria. Cytoskeletal genes appeared to have come totally from an equally ancient eukaryotic cell type. The eukaryotic cell was a product of a proto-eukaryotic cell with inputs from the other two major groups. LGT was so pervasive, however, that the exact relationship of the three groups to each other has remained elusive. Some researchers think it will still be possible to identify core genes to build a hierarchical tree of life based on vertical inheritance. Others think that rather than thinking of a tree, it is more appropriate to refer to the early history of life as a "worldwide web." The two ideas are not mutually exclusive and eventually a classification may emerge that is a synthesis of both.

Three domains or two? Or perhaps there are four or five. Various classificatory schemes have come and gone. Isn't there a certain amount of arbitrariness to classification? Objects may be classified in different ways such as shape, size, or geographical location, depending on the kind of information one is interested in retrieving. For organisms, two principles have guided the taxonomies that have developed over the centuries: similarity and genealogy. Classification was to reflect the natural order. Before Darwin, naturalists believed that God or some other eternal principle was responsible for that order. However, biologists adopted Darwin's view that a truly natural classification, one that is not arbitrary, will be an accurate representation of genealogy, in other words it will reflect who descended from whom. With the recognition of the all pervasiveness of LGT, applying the species concept to prokaryotes is virtually impossible. What was regarded as a fundamental distinction between prokaryotes and eukaryotes had no meaning phylogenetically. However, this does not mean such a distinction is not useful in particular contexts. Neither "fish" nor "dinosaurs" are phylogenetically "real" taxonomic categories. Yet even practicing biologists use such categories. This is also true for the terms prokaryote and eukaryote and there is nothing wrong with referring to bacteria and archaea as prokaryotes. Nevertheless, molecular sequencing data has revolutionized how we think about the microbial world and this in turn has profound implications for evolutionary theory in general. Woese wrote that "a biological classification is in effect an overarching evolutionary theory that guides our thinking and experimentation, and it must be structured (and that structure changed if necessary) to reflect evolutionary reality." However, many core concepts of Darwinian evolution may not be applicable to the microbial world. First, as mentioned the idea that species exist as discrete entities with more or less isolated gene pools is simply not true for microbes. It was already known that LGT occurred in bacteria usually via plasmids and was responsible for the widespread emergence of antibiotic-resistant strains. Once this had been recognized it was harnessed for use in biotechnology. Such gene swapping appears to be far more common than was thought in higher organisms as well. Second, while mutation and genetic recombination provided the variability for selection to act on and in general such change is slow and gradual, a different dynamic appears to drive bacterial evolution. Instead, because of the pervasiveness of LGT as well as engulfment of entire cells by others, whole complexes of genes can be acquired in one step resulting in major saltational changes. The Modern Synthesis enshrined Darwin's species concept as real. Natural selection acting on populations led to speciation. The higher taxonomic categories provided a way of grouping species and were somewhat arbitrary. This idea had already been undermined with the recognition that selection can act at different levels and that evolution can occur above the species level. The species concept has now been attacked from below by our increasing understanding of the evolution of early life forms and suggests that it is the highest taxonomic category that is "real." Deep in our evolutionary past three primary lineages were established that shared and swapped information and patterns of organization that eventually gave rise to the diverse and complex web of life we see today. Not only has genetic sequencing data changed how we think about the microbial world and the early evolution of life; it holds the promise for transforming the practice of medicine.

THE PERSISTENCE OF DISEASE

At the end of *The Origin* Darwin wrote, "as natural selection works solely by and for the good of each being, all corporeal and mental endowments will tend towards perfection." Yet after thousands of generations disease persists. Alzheimer's, cancer, heart attacks, diabetes, not to mention lesser afflictions such as nearsightedness and backaches, are all part of the human condition. As a result of public health measures such as proper sewage treatment and cleaning up water supplies along with the development of antibiotics and vaccines, the twentieth century saw a dramatic decrease in morbidity and mortality from infectious disease. But infectious disease is making a comeback with the emergence of new and devastating diseases such as AIDS and SARS. New antibiotic-resistant strains of pneumonia and TB along with a host of other infectious diseases are becoming more and more common. An evolutionary perspective can provide insight into the causes of disease and help guide treatment. Many symptoms are neither causes nor explanations of diseases, but are defense mechanisms our bodies have evolved to counteract disease. A cough has evolved to expel foreign material out of the respiratory tract to the back of the throat where it can be either expelled or swallowed, allowing digestive enzymes to destroy most bacteria. Complete suppression of a cough in someone with pneumonia might be a lethal treatment in some cases. Organisms are a product of their evolutionary history. Evolution creates new structures essentially by tinkering with old ones, resulting in a design that is not as optimal as it would be if the structure were created from scratch. Contrary to what Paley claimed, that no alderman had ever choked on his feast, our food goes down a tube that crosses our trachea to get to the stomach, making it quite possible for us to choke to death. It would be much better if our nostrils were located somewhere else, but developmental constraints will prevent us from evolving nostrils at the back of our neck. Choking is serious and unfortunate, but moving the trachea to the back of the throat resulted in our modern vocal tract that made articulate speech possible. Rather than mistakes in design, our body represents a compromise of different structures. Walking upright freed up our hands to do all kinds of complex manipulations, and to carry babies, food, and weapons, but also made us subject to backaches. Perhaps in another million years natural selection will have further refined our skeleton for walking on two feet instead of four.

For most of our history we have lived in the wild, in small societies as hunters and gatherers. Natural selection has not had enough time to evolve adaptations to the present environment of artificial lights, fatty diets, and automobiles. The coordinated set of changes in our body in response to stress known as "fight or flight" is a very effective adaptation for encountering a sabre-toothed tiger. It is not effective for an altercation with the boss or being in a traffic jam. All kinds of everyday stresses set off this reaction and being in this mode chronically can result in a variety of health problems. We are constantly hearing about the genetic underpinnings of disease, but many of these genes were harmless in the environment of our ancestors. Genes that are implicated in heart disease were not a problem until we started overindulging in a diet rich in fats. Many of us are carrying variants of the thrifty gene. First disovered in the Pima Indians, it was an adaptation to the irregularity of their food supply. It allowed them to store fat in times of plenty for use when food was scarce. The Pimas were like the proverbial canary in the coal mine. Years before the current obesity epidemic in the general United States population, the Pimas were already experiencing an epidemic in obesity, heart attacks and type 2 diabetes in young children because they were no longer eating their traditional diet, but rather one high in fat. This combined with more leisure time and less physical activity proved to be disastrous for them. Humans evolved in an environment where food was often scarce and those of our ancestors who had a preference for sweet fruits and foods high in fat such as nuts sought them out. They were good sources of energy and we are the result of that selection process. Most of us like the taste of fat and sweets because in the Pleistocene environment it was a selective advantage. Now in the land of plenty where we can just gorge ourselves continually this preference is no longer an advantage. Genes certainly exist that contribute to different metabolic rates, but rather than searching for "fat genes" most of us just need to eat less, eat a greater variety of foods and exercise more. Some genes, in spite of causing disease are still selected for because they confer benefits in particular environments in combination with other genes. The sickle cell gene is the best-known example of what is a seemingly deleterious gene. However, in heterozygotes it confers significant survival benefits in environments where malaria is prevalent. As the globe heats up, the prevalence of the sickle cell gene as well as other hemoglobin variants will undoubtedly increase. Some diseases may represent compromises and also have some hidden benefits. Experiments in several different animals have shown that genes that have considerable benefits in promoting reproductive success early in life also contribute to senescence. Furthermore, there is no selection pressure to eliminate genes that cause disease later in life. Natural selection selects only for traits that contribute to reproductive success. These are just a few examples of how evolutionary theory can inform our understanding of disease. Disease persists because we evolved and adapted to an environment that is quite different than the present. Traits that had high fitness in the past may contribute to reduced fitness today. A Darwinian perspective looks at both genetic and infectious diseases in the context of the evolutionary history of populations as well as the individual.

INFECTIOUS DISEASE

Where an evolutionary perspective promises to be most fruitful is in our approach to infectious disease. We have co-evolved with disease-causing organisms, but since infectious agents reproduce and evolve much faster than us, we are always a step behind. The widespread use and misuse of antibiotics in treating human disease and perhaps even more importantly in agriculture, acts essentially as a selecting agent for resistant strains. This is one of the primary reasons hospital-acquired infections are so difficult to treat. Any bug that has managed to survive an environment where strong disinfecting agents and antibiotics are being used all the time is bound to be highly resistant. The relationship between host and parasite is like an arms race without end. Biologists have named this the Red Queen principle from *Alice in Wonderland*. The Red Queen says to Alice "Now, here you see, it takes all the running you can do, just to keep in the same place." In the case of antibiotic resistance Paul Ewald suggests that we should harness the evolutionary changes in pathogens as a strategy for control rather than an impediment. Trying to develop vaccines that totally eliminate a particular pathogen is doomed to failure because of the Red Queen principle. Instead, vaccine development should target only the strains that are most virulent. This will leave behind variants that are less harmful or even benign and they will become the predominant strain. Ewald has suggested that in general disease-causing organisms will be less virulent if they are dependent on their host being mobile for transmission. For example, rhinoviruses that are responsible for the common cold are spread by sneezing and skin contact. People must be out and about for the virus to be transmitted and rhinoviruses are some of the mildest viruses known. In contrast, malaria is transmitted via mosquitoes and often makes its victims bedridden and is responsible for millions of deaths. There are exceptions such as smallpox, which remains one of the most lethal viruses known. It has no intermediate vector, but has evolved its own strategy. Lying dormant outside of a host, it can survive up to ten years, waiting for an opportunity to infect someone. Nevertheless, Ewald's ideas have been born out for many diseases. Cholera releases a toxin that causes diarrhea and can be spread in two ways. First, the bacteria can be picked up by someone who uses a bathroom, handles food, and then infects someone else. Cholera can also spread by drinking water contaminated by sewage. Since the first route depends on a mobile host Ewald predicted that more virulent strains would evolve in places that had contaminated water supplies – and that is exactly what he found. An outbreak of cholera in Peru in 1991 quickly spread throughout South and Central America. In countries such as Chile that had clean water supplies cholera evolved into a milder form whereas in Ecuador whose water was often contaminated it evolved strains of greater virulence. Cleaning up water supplies not only removes most pathogens, it creates an environment conducive to making the remaining ones evolve into more benign strains. The infamous Typhoid Mary is the exception that proves the rule. Typhoid, like cholera, causes diarrhea and is spread by ingested food or water that has been contaminated by the feces or urine of an infected person. It is also highly virulent, and has been controlled largely by cleaning up water supplies. Mary Mallon was the first person in the United States identified as a healthy carrier of typhoid. Working as a cook in New York she infected at least 53 people. She never experienced any symptoms, working for households and institutions that had outbreaks of the disease and in doing so continued to transmit the disease. Yet for the most part we do not see large numbers of people who are healthy carriers of dangerous diseases. One of the reasons Mary became infamous was her continual denial that she was infectious and her refusal to cooperate with public health officials.

Making use of the kinds of strategies Ewald suggests has started to have success in the eradication of malaria. Mosquito netting and screens prevent the mosquito from biting people at night, slowing down the transmission rate. The more virulent strains of *Plasmodium*, the parasite responsible for malaria, would be at an evolutionary disadvantage, killing off its hosts before they could infect someone else and thus milder strains can start to predominate. Limited use of nets impregnated with the pesticide DDT (dichlordiphenyltrichloroethane) has been shown to be highly effective. However, great caution must be used. When first developed, DDT was hailed as a panacea. Not only was it touted as a cure for malaria, it also killed all kinds of insects and other pests that were destroying agriculture crops. Rachel Carson warned that pesticides could cause grave harm to the environment in her now classic work *Silent Spring* and was attacked as an alarmist. However, all her predictions came true – DDT wreaked environmental havoc. Relatively quickly resistance evolved in mosquitoes and other pests, creating more crop loss than before, because other insects that had kept them in check had been wiped out. The DDT accumulated in bird shells caused them to be so weak and brittle that several species were in danger of becoming extinct, including the American bald eagle. We, along with other organisms, may be in a constant battle with various pathogens, but we have co-evolved with them over millions of years and thus we have developed strategies to deal with them. The active ingredients of many of our pharmaceuticals are derived from plants and various microbes that have their own natural antibiotics or chemicals to kill off invaders. However, organisms have never seen in their evolutionary history the vast array of chemicals that have been developed since World War II and we have no idea how they will deal with them. Often the body tries to seal them off or these chemicals accumulate in fatty tissues with disastrous results. Increased cancer rates are not just due to the fact that people are living longer and not dying off from infectious disease, but also to the fact that these chemicals are carcinogens. Finally, we live in a complex interrelationship with bacteria. There are ten times more bacteria than cells in our body and they are essential to our well-being. Referred to as the microbiome, they help digest food and provide the enzymes for a variety of necessary chemical reactions. Others produce antibiotics to fight off pathogens. The bacteria in our intestines are one of the most important components of our immune system. In 2008 a woman was wasting away from a gut infection of *Clostridium difficile.* Various antibiotics had not worked and she was literally dying. Her doctor gave her an unusual transplant: bacteria from her husband's intestines. The doctor prepared a small sample of her husband's stool mixed with a saline solution and delivered it into her colon. Some symptoms disappeared within a day and the procedure was completely curative and the infection has not returned. Each part of our body has its own ecosystem of bacteria that is unique and is crucial to our health. We do not live in a sterile environment. Thus, trying to rid our environment and ourselves of bacteria is not only virtually impossible, but also harmful. The routine use of antibacterial soaps, window cleaners and other cleaning agents, just like the inappropriate use of antibiotics, selects for resistant strains that are more likely to be pathogenic.

THE EVOLVING STORY OF HIV

Human immunodeficiency virus (HIV) is another devastating disease that continues to evolve and adapt to changing environments, and illustrates the benefits of an evolutionary approach to developing treatment. After any kind of infection our immune system mounts a many-pronged attack, harnessing a variety of different kinds of white cells to search out and destroy the invader. The immunodeficiency virus is particularly insidious as it attacks the very white cells that are responsible for fighting off an infection. Nevertheless, other white cells recognize these infected cells and destroy them along with billions of virus particles, keeping the virus at bay. However, the HIV virus mutates extremely rapidly, producing new strains. Eventually strains evolve that avert detection and quickly replace the other strains. For years host and parasite are in equilibrium, the host asymptomatic. During this period, unless they have an HIV test, those infected will not realize they are carrying HIV, and can spread the disease to countless others. Full-blown AIDS (acquired immune deficiency syndrome) emerges after the immune system has essentially been destroyed and the host becomes infected by a variety of other pathogens, unable to fight them off. Drugs that interfere with the enzymes responsible for the virus's replication slow its progression, but because of its high mutation rate new strains quickly emerge and virus levels can become quite high in a matter of weeks. Now it is possible to sequence the various strains and develop a chemical cocktail of drugs that act at several mutation sites, rotating with other combinations of drugs trying to stay one step ahead of the virus. Unfortunately, multiple drug-resistant strains have already developed. The principle of the Red Queen means it is unlikely that this kind of drug treatment will ever be entirely curative. The extremely high mutation rate is also the reason it has been so difficult to develop a vaccine. Furthermore, the cost for such treatment is prohibitive for most people, particularly in countries in Africa where HIV has been especially devastating. Nevertheless, such treatments have allowed many HIV+ people to live high-quality lives for many years.

Some researchers are tracking the origins of HIV in the hopes that this may provide guidance for treatments or a cure that otherwise might not be found. A variety of animals have their own version of immunodeficiency virus, including cats, bovines and primates; HIV is most similar to the one that infects primates, known as SIV (S for simian). Unlike humans, the primates do not appear to get sick from SIV. It may have been lethal at one time, but natural selection has left only those primates that are resistant. Scientists think that the HIV epidemic is the result of SIVs jumping from primates to humans several times. While many strains of HIV exist, they are classified into two main forms: HIV-1 found in most parts of the world and HIV-2 that is so far limited to West Africa. HIV-1 is thought to have originated from an SIV in a species of chimpanzee found in equatorial West Africa. HIV-2 is more similar to the SIV from the sooty mangabey, a monkey in West Africa than it is to HIV-1. Likewise the SIV of this monkey is more similar to HIV-2 than to SIVs of other monkeys. These monkeys are often kept as pets, as well as being hunted for food. In both cases humans became exposed as a result of coming into contact with infected blood from butchering, or perhaps being scratched and the blood entering the wounds. Research suggests that HIV-1 has crossed from chimps at least three times and from the monkeys at least six times, but most of these were evolutionary dead ends. In both cases early forms of HIV would have been poorly adapted to survive in its human hosts and probably would not have spread very far. Even if someone was infected, they lived in remote villages where population density was quite low. However, in the twentieth century population density increased dramatically. An increased demand for bush meat also brought hunters into more contact with primate blood. People were much more mobile and this allowed the virus to spread rapidly throughout Africa. As West Africa had more and more contact with the rest of the world HIV went global. We have only recently begun to fully appreciate the enormous diversity in the microbial world as well as the amazing ability of microbes to adapt to novel environments. The enormous increase in the human population and our domesticated plants and animals combined with increased mobility means that we are at increased risk for coming into contact with wild reservoirs of pathogens. We can expect to see more outbreaks of diseases such as SARS and SIH1 flu.

As devastating as HIV has been, some people although infected with HIV-1 never develop AIDS. Researchers found that individuals carrying two copies of a mutation of the *CCR5* gene did not have receptors on their CD4-T white cell surface that allowed entry of the HIV virus into the cell. These people did not become infected with HIV. This mutation is relatively common in Europe, in some populations as high as 20 percent, and then decreases in frequency in Asia and is non-existent in African populations. There must have been strong selection pressure for it to reach such a high proportion and some researchers suggested the Black Death or plague was the responsible selective force. Bubonic plague is caused by *Yersinia pestis*, which also binds to white cells. Rather than invading the cell, it injects toxins that incapacitate the cell allowing the bacteria to multiply. Descendants of those individuals who survived the plague might not have the receptors and would be protected from HIV. Other research suggests that smallpox was the selective agent responsible for the increase in the *CCR5* allele. Over the long term smallpox has killed far more people, although in less dramatic fashion and the allele was already relatively common before the first outbreaks of the plague. This example, however, shows the importance of evaluating different kinds of evidence. Based on historical, archeological and medical evidence, some researchers suggest that the Black Death was not due to bubonic plague, but some other organism, perhaps smallpox. If this turns out to be correct it would overturn a long-standing view of the cause of the Black Death. Regardless, the discovery of the *CCR5* mutation holds promise for the development of an effective treatment to prevent HIV infection. It also suggests that the devastating and widespread incidence of HIV in Africa may be due in part to differing evolutionary histories of different populations. Knowing the genetic history of different populations promises to be relevant for other diseases as well.

WHY SEX?

For billions of years all life forms reproduced asexually and today such organisms remain far more plentiful. Reproducing sexually is very inefficient. In sexually reproducing organisms only half the individuals have offspring. An asexual organism simply divides. An amoeba does not need to find a mate. It does not need to expend energy growing beautiful feathers such as the peacock to attract a mate nor engage in bloody confrontations with other amoebas to win access to a mate. Clearly sex is not only not necessary, it also has many costs. Yet sex is everywhere. Plants, animals and most single-celled organisms have evolved mechanisms that confer on them the advantages of having sex. Sex generates diversity and this is such an evolutionary advantage that it far outweighs any liabilities. Asexual organisms are totally dependent on mutation (which is generally a rare event) to create variability and in a constantly changing environment this hinders their ability to adapt. Mixing up the genetic material to create new combinations is the essence of sex and virtually all organisms have found a way to do this. Lateral gene transfer is essentially a form of sex. Paramecium, a single-celled organism that produces by binary fission, occasionally engages in a process called conjugation in which two individuals join together and exchange genetic material. Bacteria also conjugate, swapping genes via plasmids, little rings of DNA that are separate and can produce independently of the chromosomal DNA. Plasmids carry a variety of genes that offer a selective advantage under particular conditions. These include genes that confer resistance to antibiotics, that turn a bacterium into a pathogen, that code for proteins that can kill other bacteria, that can fix nitrogen, and that can break down unusual organics that can then be a source of nutrients. Even plants that often have both male and female organs have often evolved ways to prevent self-fertilization to increase genetic mixing. Variation is the key to adaptation and sex maximizes variation. This remains the primary explanation as to why sex evolved. However, an idea that is gaining increasing support is that sexual reproduction has become so prevalent because it provides an effective strategy to keep parasites in check. Organisms that reproduce clones of themselves may do quite well for a time, but since they are genetically identical, a parasite could potentially wipe out the entire population. Sexually reproducing organisms produce offspring that are each genetically unique. While some individuals would be vulnerable to a particular parasite, others would not. Over the long run sexually reproducing populations would be more stable. Mathematical modeling supports this view, but relatively few studies have shown if this is what is happening in nature.

Scientists began monitoring a species of New Zealand freshwater snail in 1994. These snails produce both asexually and sexually and the scientists kept track of the number of asexuals and sexuals and rates of parasitic infections of both groups in several different populations. While at first the clones did very well, as the years went on their rates of infection increased, their numbers decreased dramatically and some clones disappeared entirely. In contrast the sexually reproducing populations remained much more stable. The topminnow, a fish found in ponds in Mexico that is heavily para-sitized by a worm, was another natural experiment that provided evidence for the Red Queen hypothesis. Parasite and host evolved together and sexual reproduction helped maintain a stable equili-brium. As with the snails, sexual and asexual forms coexist. The asexual strains accumulated parasites at a far higher rate. What appeared to be the exception in fact proved the rule. In one of the ponds the sexually reproducing fish were heavily infested with the worm. However, closer analysis revealed that the pond had almost entirely dried up at one point and only a few fish survived to repopulate it. The fish in this pond were highly inbred, having very little genetic diversity just like their asexual cousins and likewise harbored high levels of parasites.

INFECTION AND CHRONIC DISEASE

Ewald also thinks many chronic diseases such as heart disease, arthritis and other inflammatory diseases, and even mental illnesses such as schizophrenia, may be due to infectious agents. These dis-eases, in spite of having a large negative impact on fitness, have remained quite high in the population and he thinks they are likely to be the result of infections. This has been a much more con-troversial claim, but evidence is beginning to accumulate that he might be right. Ulcers for a long time were the classic example of a psychosomatic illness. Chronic stress caused the stomach to release too much hydrochloric acid that literally digested away the lining of the stomach creating an ulcer. Although evidence existed as early as the 1940s that ulcers might be caused by an infection, it was not until the 1980s that the bacterium *Helicobacter pylori* was shown to be the culprit. It was not until the mid-1990s that it was well accepted by the medical community.

Autoimmune diseases such as multiple sclerosis and arthritis are the result of the overreaction of the immune system generating a hyperinflammatory response. The body literally attacks itself. Inflammation is virtually always an indicator of infection. The immune system is usually quite good at recognizing the difference between self and non-self. If autoimmune diseases are primarily due to genetics, then natural selection should weed them out. Yet they appear to be on the rise. The risk factors for heart disease have been diet, other lifestyle choices and genetics. Yet now chronic inflammation of the arterial walls has been implicated in the build up of plaque and the development of arteriosclerosis, putting those individuals at much higher risk for heart attack and stroke. What is the underlying cause of the inflammation? Although not definitively proven, evidence suggests that *Chlamydia pneumoniae,* a pathogen that causes acute respiratory disease, might be responsible. The antibody to it has been found in people with coronary artery disease, myocardial infarction, carotid artery disease, and cerebrovascular disease. The organism has been found in atherosclerotic lesions throughout the arterial tree and is rarely found in healthy arterial tissue. Perhaps the germ is only an innocent bystander or a secondary, opportunistic infection. However, the studies are intriguing and warrant further research. Epidemiological studies have also shown that in some cases infectious agents, particularly *Toxoplasma gondii,* may play a causative role in the development of schizophrenia. The organism must complete its life cycle in cats, but it also has intermediate hosts including humans. In animals it can affect behavior, and acute infection in humans can produce psychotic symptoms that are similar to those in schizophrenics. Several studies have shown a statistically significant difference in the presence of *T. gondii* antibodies between schizophrenics and controls. Exposure to cats in childhood is a risk factor for the development of schizophrenia. Some drugs used to treat schizophrenia also inhibit the replication of *T. gondii* in cell culture. Like heart disease, schizophrenia has a complex etiology and many factors are undoubtedly involved in the manifestation of the disease. Nevertheless, infection being the cause of schizophrenia was proposed as early as 1896. Early in the twentieth century it was recognized that syphilitic insanity was due to an infection. More carefully designed double-blind and epidemiological studies examining the role of infection in the development of mental illness need to be done.

In a somewhat ironic twist, our obsession in the developed countries of trying to rid our environment of microbes may actually be interfering with the development of a healthy immune system. There has been a dramatic increase in the incidence of severe allergic response to various foods such as nuts, wheat, and dairy products along with an increasing incidence of asthma. According to the hygiene hypothesis, exposure to microbes contributes to a rich and diverse intestinal flora that is a crucial part of the immune system. In addition, exposure also helps educate the immune system. We did not evolve in a sterile environment, and living in too clean an environment has resulted in the immune system not having enough to do. It starts attacking normally harmless antigens present in pollen or various foods. Various epidemiological studies support such an analysis. An increased incidence of asthma and allergies is associated with antibiotic use in the first year of life. Allergies, autoimmune and other immunological diseases are much more common in industrialized countries. As developing countries become more affluent and probably cleaner, an increase in immunological disorders also occurs. The incidence of immunological diseases in immigrants from the developing world to industrialized countries correlates to the amount of time they have lived in their adopted country. Other factors including genetics undoubtedly play a role in allergies, as well as increased levels of pollution, but the hygiene hypothesis is another example of the importance of evolutionary thinking in understanding disease processes.

Although still in its infancy, **Darwinian medicine** will eventually dramatically change the way we treat disease. Ironically, as we discover more and more of the genetic components of disease, the most effective way to treat disease may be by environmental intervention. Genes are not destiny. Most diseases have a complex etiology and it is often not particularly useful to try and parse exactly what is the genetic and what is the environmental component. Furthermore, the overemphasis on the genetic cause of disease has resulted in an underemphasis in looking at infectious agents as playing a significant causative role in many chronic diseases. An evolutionary perspective reminds us that diversity is the key to adaptation in an ever-changing environment. Rather than referring to many traits as design flaws or defects, a more useful approach is to regard them as quirks that are the product of our evolutionary history and are harmful only when they interact with novel environments.

FURTHER READING

Antolin, M. (2009) "Evolutionary biology of disease and Darwinian medicine," in M. Ruse, J. Travis, (eds) *Evolution: The First Four Billion Years,* Cambridge, MA: Belknap Press.

Bada J., Lazcano, A. (2009) "The origin of life," in M. Ruse and J. Travis, (eds) *Evolution: The First Four Billion Years,* Cambridge, MA: Belknap Press.

Ewald, P. (2002) *Plague Time the New Germ Theory of Disease,* New York: Anchor Press.

Fox, D. (February 2008) "Did life evolve in ice?" *Discover.*

Sapp, J. (2009) *The New Foundations of Evolution: On the Tree of Life,* New York: Oxford University Press.

WEBSITE

The Origin of Life, by Albrecht Moritz bib.talkorigins.org/faqs/abioprob/originoflife.html

7

HUMANKIND'S FUTURE
AN EVOLUTIONARY PERSPECTIVE

THE EVOLUTIONARY BASIS FOR HUMAN BEHAVIOR

As we saw in **Chapter 5**, Darwin realized that for people to accept that his theory was applicable to humans, he had to provide an evolutionary account of human behavior, specifically the moral sense. Trying to understand human behavior in terms of biology has a long history that predates Darwin. The idea that people are born with basic temperaments can be traced back to the Greeks, if not even earlier. Today, evidence from neurology, genetics, and physiology documents the enormous role biology plays in who we are as individuals. Evolution has also contributed significantly to our understanding of human nature, but many different evolutionary accounts have been told. The latest narrative comes from the field of evolutionary psychology, an extension of sociobiology. In 1975 E. O. Wilson's book *Sociobiology* examined the biological basis of the social behavior in animals. *Sociobiology* contained a vast compendium of valuable information on virtually all aspects of animal behavior. The final chapter was devoted to humans and created a storm of controversy. Wilson argued we are biological beings and that even the many diverse forms of culture were rooted in biology. If we go against our biology we do so at our own peril and thus we need to create a biology of sociology. Some critics questioned the applicability of the behavior of ants (Wilson is an expert on the social insects) or even that of other mammals to humans. This is a valid concern, but animal studies have contributed a great deal to our understanding of humans. A more serious charge, Wilson was accused of being a biological determinist, overemphasizing the role of genetics and undervaluing the role of culture in understanding human behavior. Many people did not accept Wilson's extreme reductionism, claiming that many aspects of culture (and therefore behavior) take on a life of their own and an adequate explanation does not need to turn to biology. While the term sociobiology broadly refers to all biological aspects of behavior, it has come to refer specifically to the investigation of evolutionary questions. How did a particular behavior evolve and how is it maintained? The core of Darwin's theory has not just been explaining how species change, but how they adapt. This has been evolutionary theory's greatest strength, but also its greatest weakness as an adaptive story can be told about virtually any trait. Stephen Gould and fellow Harvard evolutionary biologist Richard Lewontin have been long-time critics of what they referred to as "just-so stories," the phrase taken from Rudyard Kipling's animal stories. In a now classic paper, "The Spandrels of San Marco and the Panglossian Paradigm: A Critique of the Adaptationist Programme," they argued that many traits are not adaptations at all, but were rather developed for one purpose and are now used for another. The title of the paper comes from an architectural structure used in St Mark's basilica in Venice. The dome is perched on four arches that are at right angles to each other. Because the arches are rounded, this creates triangular space at the corners that are called spandrels or pendentives. Three hundred years later, the spandrels were decorated with beautiful mosaics. However, they were not created to provide a space for mosaics. Rather the spandrels were a by-product resulting from the design of having a dome on four arches. Using the spandrels as an analogy, Gould and Lewontin argued that just because a particular adaptive explanation was plausible does not necessarily mean it was true. They suggested that alternative explanations were not being adequately explored. For example, feathers might now be used for flying but they were probably originally an adaptation for thermoregulation. The problem is how does one tell a good adaptive story from a bad one? When it comes to human evolution, particularly behavior, this problem is severe. Yet in spite of some very contentious debates in the 1970s and 1980s, sociobiology has provided valuable insights into human behavior.

EVOLUTIONARY PSYCHOLOGY

Building on the ideas of sociobiology, evolutionary psychologists specifically want to use evolutionary theory to bridge the gap between biology and culture. Our large brain is ultimately what makes possible all the rich cultural diversity that exists in the world today. However, our brain is not a cultural artifact; it is a biological organ. One could argue that our brain is the ultimate adaptation that makes us human. Evolutionary psychologists claim that the human mind consists of a set of cognitive mechanisms, discrete modules or "organs" that evolved as adaptations to the Pleistocene environment referred to as the environment of evolutionary adaptation or EEA. The husband and wife team of John Tooby and Leda Cosmides, leaders in this field, have applied these ideas to interpret the results of a variety of psychological experiments. In the Wason test four cards are laid out that read Z, 5, E, and 6. The subject is told there is a general rule that if one side has a vowel, the other side will have an even number. Which card or cards does the subject have to turn over to see if the rule holds? The correct answer is 5 and E. Even if 6 had a consonant on the other side the rule still holds. Less than 10 percent of subjects answer this question correctly. However, when the test is changed to reflect a social situation, results dramatically improve. Now the cards have the ages of people in a bar on one side and the drinks they have ordered on the other and read 17, Sprite, 26, and Martini. Which cards have to be overturned to see that no one is breaking the law by under-age drinking? The correct answer is 17 and Martini. Virtually everyone answers this question correctly, although the underlying logic to solve it is identical to the first test. Cosmides and Tooby claim this is because we have evolved a brain that is good at keeping track of social complexities. We are also good at detecting cheating because living cooperatively as hunter gathers, it would be important that our ancestors could recognize people who were dishonest. However, the claims of evolutionary psychologists are problematic for a variety of reasons. First, we do not have the kind of detailed knowledge of the Pleistocene environment necessary to illuminate the specific behaviors that humans would have evolved to solve specific problems. All animals had to find food and mates, take care of their young, avoid predation, and a variety of other tasks. Organisms solve problems of survival in many different ways, and even within species tremendous variation in behavior exists. Gould and Lewontin's adaptationist critique remains highly relevant. Second, assuming that it is possible to eliminate the biases of gender, race, class, and cultural superiority that continue to pervade the various evolutionary scenarios being offered about the origins of our behavior, two fundamental problems underlie the whole discipline of evolutionary psychology. Just as with sociobiology, the explanatory power of evolutionary psychology depends on the belief that complex behavior is primarily genetically determined. However, this claim is highly disputed. Although the popular press continues to portray research findings in terms of nature *or* nurture along with various scientists as well, in actuality the discussion should be nature *via* nurture. As developmental psychologist Jerome Kagan wrote

> The power of genes is real but limited – a principle that operates even during the growth of the embryo. ... No human quality, physical or psychological, is free of the contribution of events within and outside the organism. Development is a cooperative mission and no behavior is a first-order, direct product of genes.
>
> (Kagan 1994, 50)

Furthermore, it has been virtually impossible to identify modules or clusters of traits, let alone think that they will be primarily under the control of one or a few genes. Although many faculty psychologists think that mental behavior is the result of several distinct psychological mechanisms and many cognitive psychologists agree with evolutionary psychologists that the brain is organized into distinct modules or organs, very little consensus exists on exactly what those modules are, beyond general ones such as a language system and a perceptual system.

Evolutionary psychology has attracted a lot of attention because it claims to provide explanations for highly interesting behaviors, particularly ones around gender differences such as sexual jealousy, aggression, homicidal tendencies, and sexual attraction. No one denies differences in behavior exist between men and women, but exactly what are those differences and how much of the difference is rooted in biology? The explanation for the war between the sexes offered by evolutionary psychologists is based on five core assumptions: (1) men are more promiscuous than women; (2) women are more interested in stable relationships; (3) men are attracted to youth and beauty; (4) women are attracted to high-status men with resources as potential mates; (5) these preferences were shaped in the EEA and haven't changed significantly. The primary evidence cited in favor of the different rates of promiscuity is the differences between gay men and lesbians. These populations are regarded as ideal study populations because they are free to act on the innermost impulses of their own sex, unencumbered by the wants and desires of the opposite sex as heterosexuals theoretically are. Prevailing stereotypes portray gay men as having hundreds of anonymous sexual encounters in bathhouses, while lesbians couple up into stable relationships. The only reason heterosexual men are not as promiscuous as gay men is because women won't let them be so. Yet how many homosexuals do not fit this pattern at all? Truly reliable surveys are hard to come by. Many homosexuals remain in the closet and the ones who are in the closet could not be so if they displayed the prevailing stereotype of their behavior. Assumptions about mate preferences are based primarily on surveys compiled by David Buss. He collected data in 37 countries, from a wide array of cultures and they consistently revealed the same pattern. Men would take up with all kinds of women, but when they were ready to settle down, they wanted a young, pretty, and virginal wife who would be faithful; and women wanted a mature, resourceful man. Even successful, financially secure women still wanted to marry men whose earning power and social status were equal to or preferably greater than their own. Females can't escape their innate preferences that were shaped in the EEA when they were tied down with an infant who they would have suckled for several years and they had to depend on their mate to bring home the mastodon. Furthermore, men will be most threatened by sexual infidelity while women will be most threatened by emotional infidelity. Virtually all cultures have elaborate mechanisms in play to keep women faithful, and women who are found to be unfaithful are beaten, made social outcasts, and often killed. According to Margo Wilson and Martin Daly, male sexual jealousy is an adaptive solution to the problem of cuckoldry avoidance. Unlike women, men cannot be absolutely sure that a child is their own and they do not want to be investing in unrelated offspring. Thus, they will go to great lengths to prevent that from happening and will be totally unforgiving if they find out that their mate has been unfaithful. Women also can be very jealous, but they will tolerate men's sexual infidelities, so long as they remain providers. They are much more threatened about an emotional attachment because this is more likely to result in a withdrawal of support, both financially and in care-taking of the children. This story offered by the evolutionary psychologists appears to provide a good explanation of observed differences between male and female behavior. However, not only is there data that contradicts this story, a variety of other stories can be told that explain the differences in male and female behavior. We do not necessarily have to look deep into our evolutionary past to find another explanation as to why women are attracted to men who make a decent wage. Men make up about half the population, but they control between 75 and 95 percent of the world's wealth. In the United States a bachelor's degree adds $28,000 to a man's salary, but only $9,000 to a woman's. Women recognize, just as their sisters have throughout history, that the best and most efficient way to accumulate status and wealth is to marry it, rather than try to achieve it on their own. Furthermore, professional women have found out that many men resent having a mate who is more successful than they are. It threatens their self-esteem and their status within the male hierarchy. Perhaps women would not be so concerned about a male's ability to earn a good living if they believed he genuinely would be pleased to have his partner be a high achiever. Furthermore, homosexuals do not corroborate the predictions of the evolutionary psychologists in regard to jealousy. Gay men are not particularly concerned about sexual fidelity, and being a good provider is a non-issue for lesbians who are generally quite egalitarian in their relationships and financial arrangements. Perhaps the most serious criticism is how could our female ancestor in the EEA of the Pleistocene "know" the differences between a sexual dalliance and a serious threat to her pair bond that would leave her and her offspring destitute? Moreover, we don't really know if our ancestors formed pair bonds, although that is a prevailing assumption in spite of not finding much support for it in the relationships of other primates.

The current theories being offered about behavior differences between men and women are very close to Darwin's original theory of sexual selection. According to Darwin males compete for females and females choose. Anything that makes the male more attractive to the female will increase his chances of getting his genes into the next generation. For example, male birds often engage in elaborate courtship rituals and have spectacular plumage while the females are often quite drab. In addition, the female is supposed to be highly discriminating or coy, while the male courts and mates with anything he possibly can. In this narrative, females could always find someone to mate with and they could afford to be choosy. This meant that there was very little variance in female reproductive success, but because of male–male competition for the attentions of the coy female, their reproductive success varied greatly. A corollary to these ideas was implicit in many of Darwin's writings, but not explicitly stated: since females were always breeding to capacity, selection acted primarily on the males. Darwin had plenty of evidence that this was the case. One only had to look at the beautiful plumes of male peacocks, the huge antlers of male deer, and the generally bigger size of males, to conclude that natural selection exerted its power primarily on the male of the species. In spite of Darwin's brilliance and his willingness to go against cherished beliefs, he could not escape his time. In many respects Darwin's theory reads as if he grafted Victorian morality onto the animal kingdom. Nevertheless, evidence for the difference in variance between male and female reproductive success was confirmed by meticulous experiments conducted by Angus John Bateman in fruit flies. Twenty-one percent of the males produced no offspring at all, but only 4 percent of the females had no offspring. In addition a successful male produced nearly three times as many offspring as the most successful female. Since it would always be to the advantage of the male to mate just one more time there would exist strong selection pressure on males to be undiscriminating and eager to mate. Because females would already be breeding close to capacity after just one copulation, they should be highly discriminating in their choice of mates and be uninterested in mating more than once or twice. There would be selection pressure on them to pick the best and strongest male to father their offspring. Robert Trivers, a leading evolutionary theorist and architect of sociobiology, built on the ideas of Bateman. Triver's evolutionary narrative has two central themes. First, the nurturing female invests much more per offspring than the male and is contrasted with the competitive male who invests little more beyond sperm, but actively competes for access to any additional females. Because the egg is so much bigger than sperm, it is energetically much more costly to make and there will be selection pressure on females to protect their eggs. Since females were already breeding close to capacity and their invest-ment was already large, it was assumed that it could not be increased. There would be little variance in female reproductive success just as Bateman's experiments showed (although one might ask why so much weight should be given to the behavior of fruit flies in building models of human behavior). Second, males were making sperm all the time with supposedly energetically little cost, and could afford to disseminate it indiscriminately. Because research showed that male reproductive success was highly variable, Trivers assumed selection pressure on males would be to engage in sex as much as possible. This story is imminently plausible. Clearly, males have the ability to inseminate multiple females while females in many species are inseminated only once during each breeding period. Yet much contradictory information was ignored. In some species of fish, insects, and cats several fathers are involved in a single brood. Moreover, not only was there no cost-accounting of how much energy it takes to make all that sperm, but more importantly the energetic costs of competing with other males for access to females were also ignored, whether it was growing bigger antlers and bigger plumes or actually engaging in fights, a common occurrence throughout the animal world.

A lot of contradictory data about female behavior was also ignored. First, it has been well documented in several different species of primates that females compete among themselves for resources, status, territory, and a variety of other factors to help ensure that they successfully raise their offspring to maturity. In baboons, reproductive success is most highly correlated with the mother's position in the female hierarchy. Second, this particular story does not provide a good explanation for the females that in the words of Sarah Hrdy "forgot to be coy." With the advances in DNA tech-nology, it is now possible to unequivocally identify paternity. Although many bird species mate for life, many female birds are less than chaste. Female cats are notoriously promiscuous. A lioness will mate up to one hundred times a day with many different males for the six- to seven-day period she is in estrous. Non-human primates engage in a wide range of mating behaviors. Female savanna baboons initiate multiple brief consortships while female chimpanzees alternate between prolonged consortships with one male and communal mating with all males. Bonobos (as closely related to humans as to chimpanzees) have sex all the time and both males and females engage in frequent homosexual acts. Finally, many critics of the mate preference surveys have pointed out that women and men are much more similar than different in what they want in a prospective partner. In every culture, both women and men rate love, dependability, emotional stability, and a pleasant personality as the four most important traits in a mate. Only in the fifth tier do the differences that the evolutionary psychologists claim are so basic emerge.

Females become pregnant and have babies; males do not. It is unlikely that natural selection would not have produced different adaptations for this most fundamental difference. However, instead of perpetuating the prevailing stereotype of coy, passive females and competitive, promiscuous males, a different evolutionary story could be told. Females take great risks to philander, but they do. Even if the evolutionary psychologists' explanation of jealousy is correct, it does not explain why female primates should be "promiscuous." There are energy costs to finding additional males to mate with. Females who wander risk the protection of one particular male, being attacked by a jealous male, having their offspring killed, and risk contracting venereal disease by having multiple partners. To even begin to address these issues means recognizing the limitation of sexual selection theory. Male–male competition and female choice would be only one aspect of a different evolutionary narrative. Additionally, genetic benefits for offspring of mothers who were sexually assertive as well as non-genetic benefits for mothers and/or progeny would be elements of the story. This narrative looks at the world from a female point of view. Hrdy suggested a variety of hypotheses as to why "promiscuous" behavior would be selected for in females. First, sperm from a number of males ensures conception. If a female has only one partner who is sterile, her genes would be lost forever to future generations. More than one father also helps ensure that offspring will have a variety of different traits, some of which will be adaptive in a constantly changing environment. In species where litters have more than one father, assorted paternity means that females may be able to enlist aid of all the males for all the offspring because the males do not know which one is their own. Finally, if a female is successful in soliciting copulation from a higher-ranking male, this could possibly result in stronger offspring. There are possible non-genetic benefits for several different hypotheses as well. Multiple matings are possibly physiologically beneficial in making conception more likely. In the "prostitution" hypothesis, females exchange sexual access for resources, enhanced status, etc. The "keep 'em around" hypothesis suggests that with the approval of the dominant male, females solicit subordinate males to discourage them from leaving the group. Finally, the "manipulation hypothesis" claims that by confusing males about the paternity of the offspring females are able to extract investment in or tolerance for their infants from different males and avoid infanticide. Human females are the only primates that have concealed estrus, and so sexual receptivity has become decoupled from estrus, making it far easier for them to manipulate males. A more complex story can be told about male behavior as well. Many benefits exist for a male who bonds with one female and invests heavily in her offspring whom he can be reasonably sure are his own. Data from non-human primates as well as cross cultural studies in human societies show that females do a great deal more than what is defined as traditional "mothering behavior" that influences the survival of their offspring. Males are more than just sperm donors and engage in a wide range of behavior that also affects the outcome of offspring. The astonishing film *The March of the Penguins* beautifully documented the importance of the male penguin in the successful raising of offspring. Females are more political and males more nurturing than traditional sexual selection theory suggests. It is apparent that many different strategies can result in reproductive success. Diversity and variety has always been and remains key to the process of evolution.

The meaning of the terms nature and culture have been heavily contested throughout history with the idea of biological determinism going in and out of vogue. By using the language of genetics and evolution, evolutionary psychologists mask the fact that there is little direct experimental evidence in favor of their theory. The evolutionary psychologists are telling a story about why humans act the way they do. A variety of factors, from the power and prestige of molecular biology to cultural attitudes about males and females, influence both the construction and evaluation of the stories. Evolutionary psychology consists of a mixture of important insights along with claims that are highly questionable. It has the potential to contribute enormously to our understanding of human behavior, but there are significant problems that must be overcome before it will be able to do so.

LANGUAGE: THE ULTIMATE ADAPTATION FOR SOCIAL ANIMALS

Perhaps the hallmark of our species is symbolic language, which in turn has made possible complex culture. The gorilla Koko and the bonobo Kanzi along with several other primate "celebrities" have learned sign language and with the help of computers have demonstrated the ability to create novel communications with their trainers. Some chimpanzees have been observed signing to other members of their troupe. Nevertheless, their communications are still very rudimentary in spite of years of intense training. Most important, they would never acquire language on their own. A human child will spontaneously acquire a huge vocabulary and learn how to communicate complex ideas by just being around other humans. For a long time many linguists thought that language was purely the product of culture acquired at a certain point in our history. However, in the 1960s linguist Noam Chomsky argued that the ability to acquire language was hard-wired into our brain. All the diverse languages shared certain universal patterns of grammar such as having verbs and subjects. Research since then has suggested that the brain does have special language organs or modules that store rules of grammar, syntax and semantics. A great deal of research has gone into understanding what those rules are and how they are acquired. Brain injuries sometimes leave very odd deficits in speech that have contributed to our understanding of how the brain is organized in regard to language. However, this research does not address when, why, and how language first arose, and theories abound.

Many researchers think language evolved quite recently, only 40,000 years ago, claiming that it could not have existed prior to the cultural explosion of the Upper Paleolithic. This is when we find in western Europe cave paintings, jewelry, more complicated tools and technologies associated with hunting and fishing as well as evidence of burials and trade. Yet others claim that too much emphasis is placed on this kind of evidence and that other indications of language such as barbed spears, the use of red pigment and evidence of trade networks can be found in Africa as early as 130,000 years ago. Biologists studying changes in the skull and also the growth in brain size put the beginnings even earlier and think that language arose gradually over a much longer period of time. Fossilized skulls of ancient hominids indicated that the parts of the larynx and throat that enable articulate speech had evolved to their present state 150,000 years ago. Some paleoneurobiologists think language emerged around 2 mya (million years ago) or even earlier. They base this on the study of endocasts, which are made from the insides of fossilized skulls and can leave imprints from the outside of the brain or cerebral cortex. They also compare the size of the brain of these ancient hominins. Broca's area of the brain is critical to speech as it coordinates the complicated movements of the tongue, larynx, and mouth that are necessary for speech. It is associated with a particular pattern of convolutions of the brain that does not exist in the great apes. Hints of the beginnings of the development of the frontal lobe speech area have been found on endocasts of fossils dated at 1.9 million years. Stone tools at this time suggest that the population was in the process of becoming right-handed, which the great apes are not. Both language and population-level right-handedness depend heavily on the left side of the brain. However, interpreting endocasts, particularly in regard to Broca's area, is very difficult, and also overall brain size is still small. Thus, the claim these early hominins had speech is highly speculative.

Many hypotheses have also been suggested as to how and why language emerged. Some researchers think that it evolved gradually from primate call systems. The gestural-origins hypothesis draws on the psychological connections between thought, speech and gesture. When humans talk they also gesture, and facial expressions along with intonation change. This also communicates important additional information, particularly emotional content. Some researchers think that language grew out of the interaction between mothers and infants. Non-human primates also convey information by gestures combined with emotional vocalizations. While chimpanzee mothers use virtually the same body language as human mothers in their interactions with their babies, only human mothers engage in "baby talk" a constant stream of melodic vocalization. This hypothesis suggests that as our ancestors lost their hair, babies could not cling on to their mothers unaided the way chimp babies do. These melodic vocalizations contributed to bonding and reassurance when mothers periodically put the baby down. Gradually natural selection resulted in changes in this mother–infant interaction that led to the first language. We know that as human infants acquire language, the tonal aspects in their "baby gibberish" appear before meaningful speech. It is thought that along with intonation they are learning underlying grammar and syntax.

THE GOSSIPING APE

An idea that has found considerably more support is Robin Dunbar's social-bonding hypothesis, nicknamed the gossiping hypothesis. Like the previous hypothesis, it focuses on why language would have evolved in the first place rather than on how language helps the exchange of information and also emphasizes how language contributes to social bonding. The anthropologist and linguist Gregory Bateson studied communication in several different mammals and emphasized that their communications were always about relationships. He maintained that what was novel about human language was that it evolved to be able to convey specific information about something other than relationships. He claimed that even after that had been achieved, it hardly affected the behavior of humans. Today a great deal of research on non-verbal communication supports Bateson's claim. Building on this idea Dunbar suggested that language developed in humans to replace social grooming which was critical to social bonding. His theory consists of four main points: (1) the size of social groups among primates correlates with the size of the neocortex; (2) for perhaps the same reasons human social networks appear to be limited to about 150 members; (3) the time spent on grooming is directly related to group size since grooming facilitates social bonding; (4) language evolved because as human groups grew larger, social grooming simply became too time-consuming, and language provided a more efficient way of conveying this important social information. Non-human primates spend an inordinate amount of time grooming each other, removing burrs, loose skin, and insects. How much time two individuals spend grooming each other correlates to how strong the bond is between them and the extent that they can count on each other for support. Dunbar argued that as group size grows, there is increased competition for social dominance and resources. One way to deal with this is to make allies and grooming provides a way of cementing these relationships. As our human ancestors moved out of the forests, they were at greater risk from predators. Forming larger groups provided increased protection from predators but at the same time made greater time demands in regard to grooming, as the size of "grooming cliques" also increased. Eventually not enough time existed to meet this increased demand and "vocal grooming" made it possible to groom several individuals at once. This allowed larger alliances to form. Individuals communicated reassurances, where they were, and what they were doing. Many non-human primates use calls to communicate this type of information to maintain alliances, which Dunbar describes as "grooming-at-a-distance." It is from this kind of vocalization that he thinks language evolved. However, even this kind of communication would eventually reach its limit. A more efficient means was necessary to create social bonding in larger sized groups. Vocalizations would start to acquire meaning, but that meaning was primarily social. As Dunbar said "Gossip had arrived." Research by Dorothy L. Cheney and Robert M. Seyfarth in vervet monkeys has shown that their calls communicate a great deal of social information in addition to location. Yet there is also a limit to how much information can be encoded in just calls. As the number of calls increases, it would become difficult to distinguish one call from another. Actual language makes it possible to escape that limitation. It facilitates other kinds of information sharing in addition to what others are doing, such as what they are saying about you. It helps evaluate whom to trust in building alliances. As we continue to learn more about the brain, not only are we learning more about the evolution of language, but about other qualities that contribute to our humanity such as kindness, justice, and empathy.

As with other capabilities, these traits are not unique to humans, but are more developed in our species.

REVISITING EVOLUTIONARY ETHICS

Evolutionary ethics has had a contentious history and again illustrates how Darwin's theory has been used to tell many different stories about both animals and humans. When *The Origin* was first published, Huxley was optimistic about the possibility of using evolution as a guide to proper behavior and a successful life. He thought that learning nature's laws and playing by them would lead to a fair and just society. Spencer also advocated applying evolutionary theory to society, espousing an ethic that became known as social Darwinism, although a more appropriate term would be social Spencerism. In 1864 Spencer wrote that economic competition resulted in the "survival of the fittest" and many people agreed. Unbridled competition would weed out the less fit and lead to an overall improvement of society. Thus, he and his followers were against any sort of safety net, poor laws or other types of public assistance to help the less fortunate members of society. Seeming to echo Huxley, in the 1880s William Sumner wrote that struggle and competition was a law of nature and that nature was entirely neutral. But following Spencer, he also wrote that nature rewarded the most fit and by redistributing those rewards, we were rewarding and promoting the survival of the less fit members of society. This might lessen inequalities, but over time it would lead to a deterioration of society. Here was a social policy, or ethic, that grounded its validity in evolutionary theory. Many people including Darwin and Huxley were appalled by such a harsh doctrine that seemed to go against basic human decency. Huxley responded to this survival-of-the-fittest mentality in his Romanes lecture entitled "Evolution and Ethics." He maintained that the "ethical progress of society depends, not on imitating the cosmic process, still less in running away from it, but in combating it." Furthermore, Huxley articulated what was the fundamental problem of evolutionary ethics. Even accepting that natural selection has evolved creatures such as ourselves with a moral sense, it does not follow that we can look to evolution to define the content of what we call moral. "As the immoral sentiments have no less been evolved, there is so far, as much natural sanction for the one as the other. The thief and the murderer follow nature just as much as the philanthropist." Thus how can evolution provide a guide as to who was good and who was not? Like many later critics such as G. E. Moore, Huxley attacked evolutionary ethics on the grounds of committing the "naturalistic fallacy." Just because nature *was* a certain way didn't mean it *ought* to be that way. Huxley's critique goes to the heart of Darwin's theory. Although Darwin thought that over time evolution resulted in progress and overall improvement, Huxley claimed that one of the great strengths of Darwin's theory was that it also explained how organisms might not progress and even become simpler. "Fittest" had the connotation of "best," but as Huxley pointed out, best in an evolutionary sense referred to best adapted to a particular environment. In some environments only bacteria survive, and are therefore the "best." Although Huxley did not explicitly mention this, fitness in strict Darwinian terms means reproductive success. But we certainly would not describe men who brutally raped and impregnated hundreds of women as either the most fit or best members of society. Huxley had plenty of other examples to support his contention that applying evolutionary principles would not necessarily bring about improvement to society. He was responding to the particular evolutionary story espoused by the social Darwinists at the time. Countering Huxley's harsh view of nature, the Russian anarchist Peter Kropotkin in *Mutual Aid* (1902) claimed that natural selection promoted group characteristics and sentiments, and that we have a natural sentiment to help each other. For Kropotkin, the fittest animals were the most sociable and sociability was the main factor that drove evolution. Kropotkin's ideas about how to improve society were completely the opposite of Spencer's, yet both men claimed that their ethics came directly out of evolutionary theory. Rather, it appears that they read their own social/political/economic views into evolutionary theory. This has been the problem that continues to beset evolutionary ethics to the present day as is evidenced by the contentious literature of sociobiology and evolutionary psychology. Yet the hope of building a naturalistic ethics grounded in evolution theory remains. As biological beings who evolved from some ape-like creature, we must take morality quite seriously, and we must build it into our theories about human behavior.

KIN SELECTION

Just like body parts, behaviors have evolved that enhance survival. While selfish behavior clearly has survival value, so does unselfish behavior, particularly in regard to offspring. Those who look after their children will undoubtedly be more successful in getting their genes into the next generation than those who don't. Nevertheless, it has been difficult to explain how altruism could have evolved. The meerkat who acts as a sentinel and loses its life warning others would not pass on its genes. Worker bees that give up their lives to protect the hive should disappear over time, but they do not. This was something that Darwin recognized was a serious problem for his theory. Darwin finally saw a way out of the dilemma. The sterile worker bees were all closely related and thus they were helping their kin, especially the queen. He thought that selection could be acting not just at the level of the individual, but also at the level of family: in other words, at the level of the group. Yet group selection has not found much support among those evolutionists who were trying to develop mathematical models that linked altruism to kin selection. In what is probably an apocryphal story, one evening in a pub Haldane was asked if he would save his brother from drowning. He supposedly answered, "I would save two brothers or eight cousins." A sibling shares half your genes while a cousin shares one eighth. Thus sacrificing your life for two brothers or eight cousins would be equivalent to saving yourself. Nevertheless, Haldane still felt that genes that lower individual fitness for the benefit of others could only spread through populations that were relatively small and were genetically related. It was not until the 1960s that W. D. Hamilton provided a rigorous mathematical account of how altruistic behavior could have evolved, which John Maynard Smith dubbed kin selection. His model showed that such behavior could evolve even if the beneficiaries were not the direct descendants of the individual and was referred to as "inclusive fitness." Known as Hamilton's rule, natural selection would favor gene(s) for altruism whenever $r \times b > c$, where r is the degree of relatedness; b is the benefit; and c is the cost of such genes. The altruist must be compensated for the cost of lowered individual fitness. Relatives *may* carry the gene for altruism as well, but the probability that they will is determined by r. Hamilton showed that cooperation and even sacrificing one's life turns out to be a good survival strategy, just as Kropotkin argued. A prime example of kin selection turned out to be Darwin's example of the social insects with their haploid–diploid system of sex determination, although Darwin had no knowledge of their genetics. In honeybees males are haploid; their genes derived entirely from the queen. Thus the male's sperm contains the male's entire genome and they will be genetically identical. Female offspring are diploid, with equal contributions from the queen and a male. If the queen mates with only one male, then on average female offspring will share 3/4 of their genes with their sisters and half their genes with their mother. They will also be more closely related to their sisters than their own offspring. In this scenario then it would be genetically advantageous for some of the female workers to forgo reproducing and help their sisters to reproduce instead and this was exactly what had happened. Most worker bees are sterile. Hamilton's work provided the theoretical foundation for much subsequent research in behavioral evolution, but contentious debates continued about human nature and evolutionary ethics. Most sociobiologists maintained that altruism was selfish, merely another way of getting one's genes into the next generation, as was demonstrated by the social insects. Critics claimed such comments blurred the distinction between ultimate explanations, which explain why a particular trait evolved and proximate explanations, which explain the mechanism and how a particular trait is being used today. When someone gives up her life to save her child, evolutionarily or in terms of the ultimate explanation, this could be described as a selfish act, but at the level of intentions or motivation, it is an unselfish act. Thus, describing it as a genuine altruistic act is appropriate, even if ultimately the origins for why people behave this way are rooted in kin selection. In addition, many people often save non-kin and act unselfishly with no thought of reciprocity or reward.

MOVING BEYOND KIN SELECTION

Recently, and surprisingly to everyone, E. O. Wilson has said he no longer thinks kin selection is the explanation for the organization of many of the social insects. Thirty years of research have shown that many species such as termites do not have the necessary genetics. Conversely, many insects that have the haploid–diploid system of sex determination such as sawflies are not social. Wilson and colleagues claim that what these societies all share are nests that have restricted access and are guarded by only a few individuals. Wilson now thinks that the distinctive reproductive system is a consequence rather than a cause of their highly cooperative social organization. Many people disagree, but increasing attention is being paid to the limitations of kin selection as the explanation for unselfish behavior. There is now a great deal of research that documents cooperation among non-kin. For instance, rats cooperate and the amount that they do so is shaped by previous experience. Stickleback fish share the risk in assessing the threat of an approaching predator. Olive baboons help each other in competing for mates. As Robert Trivers pointed out reciprocity can be a suc-cessful strategy that allows cooperation to evolve and Franz de Waal has demonstrated such behavior in many different species of pri-mates. One example concerns two capuchin monkeys, Sammy and Bias, who had learned to jointly pull a spring-loaded tray to secure food. When the tray snapped back before Bias had gotten her share she threw a tantrum. Sammy finally helped her secure the tray again so she could get her food. Both monkeys clearly understood the idea of mutual effort and the concept of reciprocity. Behaviors that previously had been explained by inclusive fitness are also being revisited and different interpretations are being offered. For example, Florida scrub jays stay home past reproductive age to help raise their siblings. Instead of an example of kin selection, this appears to be a social adaptation. By helping Dad secure a larger range, this enables the young males to cleave off a better territory for their own. Females also are able to choose better mates by adopting a sit-and-wait approach. A variety of findings all suggest that the conditions for kin selection are actually quite narrow even among genetically related individuals. It occurs when selection is weak and the fitness benefits are strictly additive. Yet this is often not the case. For instance, as cooperators become more common in a society, the benefits of being a cheater also rise. Cooperation that involves activities where reciprocity is delayed are especially sus-ceptible to cheaters because there is always the possibility that the behavior may never be reciprocated. Thus for cooperation to evolve that entails delayed reciprocity, there must be a level of trust and also a means of cost-accounting that keep cheaters in check. This can happen by means of social interactions, which are totally independent of kin selection. When de Waal changed the experimental design so that only one capuchin received the food, he usually shared it. If he did not, the other monkey soon went "on strike" and refused to cooperate in obtaining the food. Vampire bats share blood to help those who might not have fed on a particular night. However, repeat "beggers" will eventually be denied if they have not reciprocated. Cooperation is maintained by peer pressure. These kinds of studies suggest that the genocentric view that has dominated the thinking surround the evolution of social behavior is giving way to a more complex and nuanced view. Researchers are incorporating the great lesson that evolution teaches. Diversity in research approaches and interpretation is the best way to move the field forward.

De Waal maintains that there is a long evolutionary history of selection for traits such as cooperation, kindness, empathy, and justice. We can see the origins of right and wrong in primate behavior. Chimpanzees exhibit such traits as attachment, nurturance, empathy, and special treatment of the disabled or injured. Chimpanzee society has its own set of rules that are internalized and will result in punishment if broken. They have concepts of giving, trading, and revenge. They exhibit peacemaking behavior and moralistic aggression against violations of reciprocity. In short, they exhibit traits that provided the basis for building a moral code. In *The Age of Empathy* de Waal presents evidence that monkeys have a sense of fairness. In an experiment two capuchin monkeys are in cages side by side so they can see each other. They are trained to give the researcher a pebble and in return they each receive a cucumber slice, which they are both very happy with. One monkey starts receiving a grape instead, considered a higher quality snack because it is sweet. It doesn't take very long before the other monkey starts dropping the cucumber, then starts throwing it and finally totally refuses to participate in the experiment and sits in the back of the cage. Skeptics claim the monkeys are just showing greed and envy. But greed and envy are counterparts to justice. If one doesn't have a sense of being short-changed and entitled to more, then why would one feel envious? Examples of trust also exist in the animal world. In an old-fashioned zoo a monkey was kept in the same enclosure as a hippo. After the hippo had eaten his fill the little monkey would approach him and tap on his mouth. It was as if the monkey was a dental hygienist. The hippo opened his mouth wide and the monkey would pull out the food remains. The hippo seemed to not mind at all and kept his mouth open as long as the monkey continued his job. Hippos are not carnivores, but this was still a great act of trust. We also see this in other animals too. Cleaner Wrasses fish feed on ectoparasites of much bigger fish that could easily eat them.

Mimicry is particularly crucial to learning in primates. In a series of cleverly designed experiments de Waal demonstrated that chimpanzees needed to actually see another chimpanzee opening a box by either sliding a door or lifting it for them to learn how to do it. With a "magic" box where the door moved invisibly, no matter how many times they watched it, the chimps never learned how to do it themselves. We mimic those whom we identify with and that in turn strengthen the bonds. Newborn humans will stick out their tongues in response to their mother sticking out her tongue. Human mothers and children play games of clapping hands together or against each other in the same rhythm. These are games of synchronization. Dancing is also a way of being in synchronization. Other examples of in sync phenomena are seen in the singing of birds, and the howling of monkeys and wolves. We are now beginning to understand the neural underpinnings of this behavior and the importance of it to the development of empathy.

NEUROBIOLOGY AND THE EVOLUTION OF EMPATHY

Evidence from a variety of different sources suggests that we are hard-wired for kindness. Animal and human cognition depends very heavily on the body–brain interaction. The brain is not just a computer ordering the body around, but rather the body–brain relationship is a two way street, the body informing the brain as well. In *Descartes' Error,* neurobiologist Antonio Damasio argues that the mind–body dualism of Descartes has impeded the understanding of the mind, the brain and the nature of consciousness. The brain along with other organs of the body constitutes an integrated organism. It is the whole organism that interacts with the environment. Until relatively recently, most descriptions of human evolution have emphasized the growth of our intellectual capabilities, paying relatively little attention to the changes in our emotions that have accompanied a bigger brain. Emotions are associated with instinct and a prevailing bias has been that as our brain got bigger and more specialized we had greater control over instincts and emotions. Rationality is pitted against emotion as we are constantly told not to make decisions based on our emotions. Damasio has made a compelling case that emotions are critical to "rational" decision-making. Particular areas of the brain that are associated with emotions when damaged often result in highly irrational and destructive behavior. People with autism often score very high on standard IQ tests, yet their social interactions are often very poor and this interferes with their ability to navigate the world. It hinders them in their ability to make good decisions.

MIRROR NEURONS

The importance of emotion and the role of mimicry in the development of empathy has found additional support with the discovery of mirror neurons. In 1995 Giacomo Rizzolatti and co-workers discovered a group of neurons in the brains of monkeys that were activated not only when an action is performed, but also when the observer watched another perform an action. For example, these neurons fired not only when a monkey reached for a peanut, but also while watching another monkey grasp a peanut. In a provocative essay neurobiologist V. S. Ramachandran claimed that mirror neurons made imitative learning possible and were the driving force behind what he called the "Great Leap Forward" in human evolution. He predicted that mirror neurons will do for psychology what DNA did for biology: they will provide a unifying framework and help explain a host of mental abilities that have remained mysterious and inaccessible to experiments. He suggested that a sophisticated mirror neuron system made possible the emergence of protolanguage that was facilitated by mapping phonemes onto tongue movements. Eventually this led to a "theory of other minds," and the ability to "adopt another's point of view." By providing the neural substrate for reading another's intentions these cells could play a crucial role in the development of empathy and he dubbed them empathy or Dalai Lama neurons. They were "dissolving the barrier between self

and others." In saying this Ramachandran was not being metapho-
rical. The neuron in question simply doesn't know the difference
between self and others. Although this essay was somewhat speculative, a lot of hard data has been accumulating supporting his
ideas. These neurons fire not only when someone is poked by a
needle, but also when she watches someone else being poked.
Since they were first discovered in monkeys, this is another indication that empathy is not unique to humans. It is hard-wired into us.
We don't decide to be empathic, we simply *are*. Neurons normally
involved in a person's own sense of disgust are also activated when
the person sees other people displaying disgusted facial expressions.
Mirror neurons are also less active when study subjects are just
watching an image of an object, for example a hand picking up a
coffee cup, than when the cup is part of a social situation, such as a
table set for a party or a messy table that needs to be cleared up.
This suggests that the mirror neurons respond not merely to
another person's action, but to the intention behind that action.
Defects in the mirror neuron system have been associated with
autism and autistics often lack the ability to read another person's
intentions.

The discovery of mirror neurons suggests that awareness of others
evolved before awareness of self and that self-awareness may just be
a by-product of the awareness of others. In terms of basic survival
this makes a lot of sense as one needs to be aware and to react to
her environment. Obviously, simply awareness of others is not
empathy. However, empathy would have great survival value, first
in the caring of offspring, but also in reading the intentionality of
others in a group. This has a down side as well, making possible
manipulation and deception. The true psychopath has a very finely
honed ability to read others and then uses that skill for nefarious
purposes. Our big brain has made us capable of the greatest acts of
kindness and also of evil unknown in the rest of the animal world.
A cat is not going to blow up the world or launch a terrorist attack.

Evolution builds on what has come before and a certain amount
of aggressiveness and competitiveness has great survival value.
However, cultivating empathy also has great survival value. It is
actually showing enlightened self-interest. The whole growth of
civilization is the product of realizing that we are better off working
together. Empathy binds individuals together and makes us all have

a stake in society. Dawkins has moved considerably from his original writings, acknowledging that unselfish behavior is much more widespread and occurs in a much wider range of conditions than what it originally evolved for; i.e. it enjoys motivational autonomy. Nevertheless, behaviors have evolved that enhance survival and thus ethical premises are products of the particular history of our species. They are deeply rooted, and while human behavior is very flexible, it has strong genetic underpinnings. Yet it is possible to change ethical laws at the deepest level in the ongoing struggle to stay adapted to an ever changing environment. One of the implications of evolutionary ethics is that there can be no absolute, objective standard of morality that is eternal. Our species might eventually evolve rules that we consider morally abhorrent. Does this mean that we are doomed to a moral relativity? This recent research in neurobiology, on the limitations of kin selection and altruism, and extensive studies on non-human primates all suggest the answer is no. The possibility of building an ethics rooted in biology seems more promising. Not only do animals exhibit behaviors that provide evidence for the evolution of ethics, but also the ethics of evolution is not contrary to our own ethical sensibilities. However, not only must nature be interpreted, every human act results from a complex interaction of nature and culture. In that regard Huxley's fundamental message in *Evolutionary and Ethics* is not historically contingent. It is an eloquent and compelling reminder that great caution must be exercised in evaluating any ethical system.

THE FUTURE

Our species *Homo sapiens* has existed for only about 200,000 years and for most of that history we have lived as hunters and gatherers, which ensured that population density remained relatively low and our ecological footprint was relatively small. But even our early ancestors were responsible for the demise of hundreds of species and increasing evidence points to humans being the major factor in the extinction of the mega fauna such as the mammoth and other large organisms. The development of agriculture dramatically changed our environmental impact. The genetic modification of organisms, particularly grasses creating the rice, wheat, barley, and other grains that we are dependent on today, allowed us to expand from at most a few million people to now over 6 billion. With the development of civilization and our sophisticated technologies one species has altered the biosphere in ways never before seen in the whole history of life. While the invention of photosynthesis profoundly altered the composition of the atmosphere, the changes were the product of innumerable different species. We have altered the landscape in ways that are equivalent to changes brought by volcanoes and floods, earthquakes and ice ages. We have polluted the atmosphere and are running out of fossil fuels. We have created weapons capable of destroying all complex forms of life. What is our future? Evolution is a story of species adapting, eventually becoming a new species or going extinct. Why should humans be any different? We don't know the answer to this question, but we are a species that has evolved culture, which in turn is also evolving. We have created symphonies and poetry, built skyscrapers and sent people to the moon. We are at the edge of creating artificial life. Computers are extending the capacity of our brain and some researchers in artificial intelligence think in the near future computers will be capable of emotion and have consciousness. The World Wide Web already has created a kind of global consciousness. Perhaps the future of humanity is a cyborg. These new beings will not just be a combination of tissue and wire, but thinking, reasoning, spiritual systems whose minds are interconnected throughout the universe. We do not know what we might evolve into, but Darwin should have the last word of this magnificent process. From the end of *The Origin*:

> Thus, from the war of nature, from famine and death, the most exalted object which we are capable of conceiving, namely, the production of the higher animals directly follows. There is grandeur in this view of life, ... whilst this planet has gone cycling on according to the fixed law of gravity, from so simple a beginning endless forms most beautiful and most wonderful have been and are being evolved.

FURTHER READING

Allchin, D. (February 2011) "The domesticated gene," *American Biology Teacher*.
Barkow, J., Cosmides, L., Tooby, J. (ed.) (1992) *The Adapted Mind: Evolutionary Psychology and the Generation of Culture*, New York: Oxford University Press.

Damasio, A. (1994) *Descartes' Error: Emotion, Reason, and the Human Brain*, New York: Avon Books.

de Waal, F. (2009) *The Age of Empathy*, New York: Harmony Books.

Elman, J. *Grey Matters: Understanding Language.* Online. Available <bib.youtube.com/watch?v=K1pbnWcabMY>

Falk, D. (2009) "Evolution of language," in M. Ruse and J. Travis (eds) *Evolution: The First Four Billion Years,* Cambridge, MA: Belknap Press.

Grace, R. (2004) "Reflections on the evolution of human language: Robin Dunbar's social bonding hypothesis." Online. Available <bib2.hawaii.edu/~grace/dunbar.html>

Hrdy, S. B. (1999) *Mother Nature,* New York: Pantheon Books.

Huxley, T. (1893, 2006) *Evolution and Ethics and Other Essays*, New York: Barnes & Noble.

Ramachandran, V. S. (2000) "Mirror neurons and imitation learning as the driving force behind 'the great leap forward' in human evolution," *Edge: The Third Culture,* 1 June. Online. Available <www. edge.org>

——(2007) "The neurology of self-awareness," *Edge: The Third Culture,* 8 January. Online. Available <www. edge.org>

Sober, E., Wilson, D. S. (1998) *Unto Others: The Evolution and Psychology of Unselfish Behavior,* Cambridge, MA: Harvard University Press.

WEBSITES

Edge: The Third Culture www.org.edu

Evolution of Morality http://evolutionofmorality.net

GLOSSARY

Adaptation   (1) A character favored by natural selection because of its effectiveness in its particular role, which usually, but not always increases reproductive success. (2) The process by which an organism adjusts to a changing environment.

Allele   A variant of a gene.

Allopatric speciation   The formation of new species by physical or geographic isolation.

Anagenesis   Speciation due to the accumulation of changes in a single species in contrast to cladogenesis or branching speciation.

Analogous   Similarity that is not due to common descent.

Archaeopteryx   A very primitive reptile-like fossil bird discovered in 1861.

Archaea   The group of single-celled organisms that are distinct from bacteria and eukaryotes and are one of the three major kingdoms.

Argument from design   The observed order in the universe was evidence for the existence of a creator.

Bacteria   Prokaryotes that are genetically distinct from Archaea and are one of the three major kingdoms.

Biodiversity   The variety of life on earth, but often refers to the diversity found in a particular habitat or ecosystem.

Catastrophism   The theory that the earth's crust was primarily shaped by sudden, short-lived, violent events that were sometimes worldwide in scope.

Chronospecies   Usually applied to the fossil record, referring to a species that has changed sufficiently over evolutionary time that it is no longer considered to be the same species it was derived from.

Cladogenesis   Speciation caused by splitting of a single species into two non-interbreeding species.

Codon   A sequence of three adjacent bases in mRNA that specifies a particular amino acid.

Convergent evolution   The evolution of similar forms by two different lineages that do not share a common ancestor such as wings in butterflies and bats.

Darwinian medicine   Applying an evolutionary perspective to the understanding of health and disease.

Deep time   The concept of geologic time, and that the earth is billions of years old.

Development   The process by which an embryo changes into a mature organism.

Diploid   A cell that has two copies of each chromosome.

Dominant gene   An allele that affects the phenotype with only one copy.

DNA   The hereditary material deoxyribonucleic acid. It consists of two long-chain molecules held together by hydrogen bonding forming a double helix. Each chain contains a sequence of four nitrogen-containing bases: adenine (A), thymine (T), guanine (G), and cytosine (C).

Embryology   The study of the formation, early growth and development of living organisms.

Epigenesis   The idea that the embryo develops or unfolds from the successive differentiation of an originally undifferentiated structure.

Epigenetic   Inherited change that does not involve a change in the DNA sequence such as DNA methylation.

Eugenics   The improvement of the genetic constitution of populations (usually applied to humans) by selective breeding.

Eukaryote   The group of organisms that contain a distinct nucleus.

Evo-devo   Evolutionary developmental biology, which is integrating the study of evolution and embryology of different organisms.

Evolution   Change through time resulting in a change of allele frequency in a population.

Evolutionary ethics The use of evolutionary theory in understanding the psychology and behavior of humans to develop a system of ethics based on that understanding.

Extinction The end or dying out of a species.

Fossil The mineralized remains of once-living organisms.

Gene A sequence of DNA that specifies the amino acid sequence of a polypeptide.

Genetic drift Relative change of gene frequency due to random fluctuations, independent of natural selection; often happens in small populations.

Genotype The genetic make-up of an individual.

Germ plasm The gametes or sex cells of an organism.

Great chain of being The belief that everything in nature is organized in a hierarchy, from inanimate objects at the bottom to God at the top.

Hardy–Weinberg equilibrium A state in which genotype frequencies and ratios remain constant from generation to generation due to random mating in the absence of mutation, migration, natural selection or random drift.

Heterozygous Carrying two different alleles for the same gene.

Homeotic gene Genes that, when mutated, cause body parts to appear in the wrong places.

Hominidae The family that includes gorillas, chimpanzees, bonobos, humans and their ancestors.

Homininae The subfamily that includes all species extant or extinct that are more closely related to humans than our closest living relatives, chimpanzees or bonobos.

Hominid or **Hominin** A species that is part of the Homininae, i.e. in that branch of the evolutionary tree that gives rise only to humans.

Homology Anatomic structures or behavioral traits in different organisms that originated from a shared common ancestor.

Homoplasmy The generation of the same state by different means or convergent evolution.

Homozygous Carrying identical alleles for the same gene.

Homologous Characters that share a common ancestor.

Hypothesis A proposed explanation for an observation, phenomenon or scientific problem that can be tested by further investigation and/or experimentation.

Instinct   An inborn behavior pattern characteristic of a species and often a response to specific stimuli.

Intelligent design   A religious idea that rejects natural selection and claims that the order and complexity of the universe could only be the product of an intelligent designer such as God.

Lamarckian inheritance   The idea that an acquired trait can then be inherited.

Lateral gene transfer   Process by which genetic material is incorporated into another organism that is not the offspring of the organism; LGT is thought to be a major process in the early history of life.

Macroevolution   Evolution at or above the species level.

Meiosis   A form of cell division that produces gametes (eggs or sperm), halving their chromosome number.

Microevolution   Evolution at the level of the population.

Mirror neuron   A neuron that fires when an animal either performs an action or observes another animal performing the action.

Mitosis   The process of cell division in which a eukaryotic cell produces two genetically identical daughter cells.

Modern Synthesis   Also referred to as neo-Darwinian synthesis. In the 1940s the findings of genetics, paleontology, systematics, and a variety of other disciplines providing the modern account of evolutionary theory.

Molecular clock   Based on the theory that specific sequences in the DNA or the protein that it codes for mutate at a constant rate and can be used to determine when two lineages have diverged from a common ancestor.

Monogenesis   The theory that all human races were descended from a common ancestor and were one species.

Morphology   The form or structure of an organism or its parts.

Multiregional hypothesis   The hypothesis that our earliest ancestors radiated out of Africa and several different populations of *Homo erectus* in different parts of the world simultaneously evolved into *Homo sapiens*.

Mutation   A change (addition, deletion or substitution) in the sequence of bases in the DNA.

Natural selection   The process by which heritable traits that contribute to the survival and reproductive success of individuals become more frequent in the population, resulting in the population evolving.

Natural theology   Evidence for the existence of God that can be found through the study of nature rather than revealed religion.

Neutral theory   The theory that most of evolutionary change at the molecular level is due to genetic drift of selectively neutral mutations.

Ontogeny   The developmental history of an individual from the embryo to an adult.

Out-of-Africa hypothesis   The theory that anatomically modern humans all descended from a single African population dating about 60,000 to 100,000 years ago, replacing all other hominid populations.

Paleontology   The study of ancient life by means of collecting and analyzing fossils.

Phenotype   The appearance of an organism that results from the interaction between genes and the environment.

Phylum   A taxonomic category that is below kingdom and above class.

Phyletic gradualism   The idea that most evolutionary change is slow and occurs within a single lineage. This is contrasted with punctuated equilibrium.

Phylogeny   The evolutionary history of the species.

Plasmid   Small circular DNA that is distinct from the organism's chromosomal DNA.

Pleiotropy   Genotypes that have multiple expressions.

Polygenesis   The theory that the human races were descended from different ancestors, and thus could be considered different species.

Polymorphism   The existence of two or more variants of a trait that exist in significant frequency in a population.

Polyploidy   Having more than the usual diploid number of chromosomes.

Preformation   The theory that an organism is fully formed at conception and subsequent development is just a matter of growth.

Prokaryote   Single celled organisms that do not have a distinct nucleus or other organelles (archaea and bacteria).

Proteomics   The branch of genetics that identifies and studies all the proteins expressed by a genome.

Punctuated equilibrium The theory that claims the fossil record shows that most change occurs rapidly at the time of branching or speciation and then exhibits little change or stasis. This is contrasted with phyletic gradualism.

Purine A class of base that includes adenine and guanine

Pyrimidine A class of base that includes thymine and cytosine.

Recapitulation The theory that the development of an embryo passes through analogous stages as the species pass through its evolutionary history.

Recessive trait Must have two copies of the same allele for it to be manifested in the phenotype or if the other copy is missing.

RNA Ribonucleic acid is an informational molecule that is the intermediary between DNA and protein and exists in several forms: messenger RNA (mRNA) specifies the specific amino acid sequence of a protein; transfer RNA (tRNA) brings the correct amino acid to a mRNA codon; ribosomal RNA (rRNA), which is found on ribosomes and is part of the cell machinery to make proteins.

RNA world The theory that the first genetic material was RNA.

Saltation A leap or jump suggesting that new species or races arise abruptly rather than by slow small changes.

Scala naturae Often referred to as the great chain of being, this was a classical and medieval concept that the universe was organized in a strict hierarchy reflecting God's plan.

Segregation Referring to the separation of the hereditary units or genes in meiosis.

Species A taxonomic category that refers to a group of similar individuals that can interbreed with one another, but not with others or in asexual organism that share specific characteristics.

Spontaneous generation The theory that life can form spontaneously from non-living matter.

Stochastic process A statistical process involving a number of random variables.

Stromatolites Laminated rocks that are usually formed by the action of blue-green algae, indicative of the oldest forms of life that have been found.

Theory An explanation of observed and experimental evidence of natural phenomena that also has predictive power.

Tiktaalik   A lobe-finned fish that lived about 375 million years ago and represents a transitional organism between fish and land-based animals.

Tetrapod   A four-limbed vertebrate.

Transcription   Using DNA as a template to make an mRNA molecule.

Translation   The process by which the information from mRNA is used to make a polypeptide.

Transmutation   A term common in the nineteenth century, referring to the change or evolution of one species into another.

Uniformitarianism   The theory that the earth's crust was shaped by the same geologic processes operating uniformly from the past to the present day.

BIBLIOGRAPHY

Achenbach, J. (October 2010) "Australia's lost giants," *National Geographic*.

Allchin, D. (February 2011) "The domesticated gene," *American Biology Teacher*.

Altmann, J. (1997) "Mate choice and intrasexual reproductive competition: Contributions to reproduction that go beyond acquiring mates" in P. Gowaty (ed.) *Feminism and Evolutionary Biology: Boundaries, Intersections, and Frontiers*, New York: Chapman & Hall.

Baer, K. E. von ([1828] 1853) "Philosophical fragments *Uber Entwickelungsgeschichte The Fifth Scholium*," in A. Henfrey and T. Huxley (eds) *Scientific Memoirs, Natural History*, London: Taylor & Francis.

Barkow, J., Cosmides, L., Tooby, J. (eds) (1992) *The Adapted Mind: Evolutionary Psychology and the Generation of Culture*, New York: Oxford University Press.

Barrett, P. (ed.) (1974) *Metaphysics, Materials and the Evolution of Mind*, Chicago: University of Chicago Press.

Barthlomew, M. (1973) "Lyell and evolution: An account of Lyell's response to the prospect of an evolutionary ancestry for man," *British Journal of the History of Science* 6: 261–303.

Bateson, G. (1972) *Steps to an Ecology of Mind*, New York: Ballantine Books.

Bowler, P. (2009) *Evolution*, 4th edn, Berkeley: University of California Press.

Brockman, J. (ed.) (2008) *Science at the Edge*, New York: Union Square Press.

Brooke, J. H. (1991) *Science and Religion: Some Historical Perspectives*, Cambridge: Cambridge University Press.

Browne, J. (1995) *Charles Darwin: Voyaging*, Princeton: Princeton University Press.

——(2003) *The Power of Place*, Princeton: Princeton University Press.

Buckland, W. (1837) *Geology and Mineralogy Considered with Reference to Natural Theology,* Philadelphia: Carey, Lea & Blanchard.

Burkhardt, F., Smith, S. (eds) (1987) *The Correspondence of Charles Darwin 1844–1846,* vol. 3, Cambridge: Cambridge University Press.

Buss, D. (1989) "Sex differences in human mate preferences: Evolutionary hypotheses tested in 37 cultures," *Behavioral and Brain Sciences* 12: 1–49.

——(1995) "Psychological sex differences," *American Psychologist* 50(3): 164–68.

Campbell, L. A., Kuo, C. C., Thomas Grayston, J. T. (1998) "*Chlamydia pneumoniae* and cardiovascular disease," *Emerging Infectious Diseases* 4: 3 (Synopses). Online. Available <bib.cdc.gov/ncidod/eid/vol4no4/campbell >

Caroll, S. (2006) *Endless Forms Most Beautiful: The New Science of Evo Devo,* New York: W. W. Norton.

Carson, R. (1964) *Silent Spring,* New York: Fawcett Crest.

Cartmill, M., Pilbeam, D., Isaac, G. (1986) "One hundred years of paleo-anthropology," *American Scientist* 74(4): 410–20.

Chambers, R. ([1844] 1969) *Vestiges of the Natural History of Creation,* Leicester: Leicester University Press.

Charlesworth, B, Lande, R., Slatkin, M. (1982) "A neo-Darwinian commentary on macroevolution," *Evolution* 36: 474–98.

Cloninger, C. R., Syrakic, D. M., Przybeck, T. R. (1993) "A psychobiological model of temperament and character," *Archives of General Psychiatry* 50: 975–90.

Cohn, Jr, S. K., Weaver, L. T. (2006) "The Black Death and AIDS: CCR5-32 in genetics and history," *QJM: An International Journal of Medicine* 99(8): 497–503. Online. Available <http://qjmed.oxfordjournals.org/content/99/8/497.full>

Coleman, W. (1962) "Lyell and the reality of species," *Isis* 53: 325–38.

——(1976) "Morphology between type concept and descent theory," *Journal of History of Medicine* 31: 149–75.

——(1977) *Biology in the Nineteenth Century: Problems of Form, Function, and Transmutation,* Cambridge: Cambridge University Press.

Cosmides, L., Tooby, J. (1994) "Origins of domain specificity: The evolution of functional organization," in L. Hirschfeld and S. Gelman (eds) *Mapping the Mind* Cambridge: Cambridge University Press.

Damasio, A. (1994) *Descartes' Error: Emotion, Reason, and the Human Brain,* New York: Avon Books.

Darwin, C. ([1839] 2001) *The Voyage of the Beagle,* New York: Modern Library.

——([1859] 1976) *The Origin of Species,* 1st edn, New York: Avenel.

——([1871] 1981) *The Descent of Man,* Princeton: Princeton University Press.

——([1872] 1965) *The Expression of the Emotions in Man and Animals,* Chicago: University of Chicago Press.

——(1892) *Animals and Plants under Domestication,* 2nd edn, New York: D. Appleton & Co.

——(1887) *Life and Letters of Charles Darwin*, 2 vols, ed. F. Darwin, London: John Murray.

——(1903) *More Letters of Charles Darwin*, 2 vols, ed. F. Darwin and A. C. Seward, London: John Murray.

——(1958) *The Autobiography of Charles Darwin and Selected Letters*, ed. F. Darwin, New York: Dover.

Dawkins, R. (1976) *The Selfish Gene*, New York: Oxford University Press.

Dennett, D. (1995) *Darwin's Dangerous Idea*, New York: Simon & Schuster.

Desmond, A. (1989) *The Politics of Evolution,* Chicago: University of Chicago Press.

——(1994) *Huxley: The Devil's Disciple,* London: Michael Joseph.

Desmond, A., Moore, J. ([1991] 1994) *Darwin: The Life of a Tormented Evolutionist,* New York: W. W. Norton & Co.

de Waal, F. (1996) *Good Natured*, Cambridge, MA: Harvard University Press.

——(2009) *The Age of Empathy*, New York: Harmony Books.

Diamond, J. (1997) *Guns, Germs and Steel,* New York: W. W. Norton & Co.

Dobzanksy, T. (1937) *Genetics and the Origin of Species,* New York: Columbia University Press.

Eldredge, N. (2005) *Darwin: Discovering the Tree of Life*, New York: W. W. Norton & Co.

Eldredge, N., Gould, S. (1972) "Punctuated equilibria: An alternative to gradualism," in T. Schopf (ed.) *Models in Paleobiology*, San Francisco: Freeman, Cooper & Co.

Epstein, S. (30 March 2001) "Infection and atherosclerosis," *Medscape* CME. Online. Available <http://cme.medscape.com/viewarticle/416495>

Ewald, P. (2002) *Plague Time: The New Germ theory of Disease*, New York: Anchor Press.

Farber, P. (1976) "The type-concept in zoology," *Journal History of Biology* 9: 1: 93–119.

Fichman, M. (2004) *An Elusive Victorian: The Evolution of Alfred Russel Wallace,* Chicago: University of Chicago Press.

Fox, D. (February 2008) "Did life evolve in ice?" *Discover*.

Goldschmidt, R. ([1940] 1982) *The Material Basis of Evolution,* New Haven: Yale University Press.

Goodwin, B. (1994) *How the Leopard Changed Its Spots*, New York: Charles Scribner's Sons.

Gould, S. (1977) *Ontogeny and Phylogeny*, Cambridge, MA: Harvard University Press.

——(1977) "The eternal metaphors of paleontology," in A. Hallam (ed.) *Patterns of Evolution*, Amsterdam: Elsevier.

——(1982) "Piltown revisted," in *The Panda's Thumb,* New York: W. W. Norton & Co.

Gould, S., Eldredge, N. (1977) "Punctuated equilibria: The tempo and mode of evolution reconsidered," *Paleobiology* 3: 115–51.

Gould, S., Lewontin, R. (1978) "The spandrels of San Marco and the Panglossian paradigm: A critique of the adaptationist programme," *Proceedings of the Royal Society of London B: Biological Sciences* 205: 581–98.

Grace, R. (2004) "Reflections on the evolution of human language: Robin Dunbar's social bonding hypothesis." Online. Available <bib2.hawaii.edu/ ~grace/dunbar.html>

Granthan, T., Nichols, S. (1999) "Evolutionary psychology: Ultimate explanations and Panglossian predictions," in V. Hardcastle (ed.) *Where Biology Meets Psychology: Philosophical Essays,* Cambridge, MA: MIT Press.

Greene, J. (1981) *Science, Ideology, and World View,* Berkeley: University of California Press.

Gupta, R. S. (2000) "The natural evolutionary relationships among prokaryotes," *Critical Reviews in Microbiology* 26(2): 111–31.

Hall, B. (ed.) ([1994] 2001) *Homology: The Hierarchical Basis of Comparative Biology*, New York: Academic Press.

Haraway, D. (1989) *Primate Visions,* New York: Routledge.

Hartl, D., Clark, A. (2007) *Principles of Population Genetics*, 4th edn, MA: Sinauer Associates, Inc.

Hrdy, S. B. (1981) *The Woman That Never Evolved,* Cambridge, MA: Harvard University Press.

——(1986) "Empathy, polyandry, and the myth of the coy female," in R. Bleier (ed.) *Feminist Approaches to Science*, New York: Pergamon.

——(1999) *Mother Nature,* NewYork: Pantheon Books.

Hull, D. (1988) *Science as a Process,* Chicago: University of Chicago Press.

Huxley, J. (1942) *Evolution: The Modern Synthesis,* London: George Allen & Unwin.

Huxley, T. (1854) "Vestiges of the Natural History of Creation tenth edition, London, 1853," *British and Foreign Medico-Chirurgical Review* 13: 425–39.

——(1877) "The Demonstrative Evidence of Evolution," *Popular Science Monthly* 10: 285–98.

——(1887) "The Reception of the 'Origin of Species'," in F. Darwin (ed.) (1900) *Life and Letters of Charles Darwin,* 2 vols, New York: D. Appleton & Co.

——(1893a) *Methods and Results,* vol. 1 of *Collected Essays,* London: Macmillan & Co.

——(1893b) *Darwiniana,* vol. 2 of *Collected Essays*, London: Macmillan & Co.

——([1893] 2006) *Evolution and Ethics and Other Essays*, vol. 9 of *Collected Essays*, New York: Barnes & Noble.

——(1898) *Man's Place in Nature*, vol. 7 of *Collected Essays*, New York: D. Appleton & Co.

——(1898–1902) *Scientific Memoirs of Thomas Henry Huxley*, 4 vols, ed. M. Foster and E. Ray Lancaster, London: Macmillan & Co.

——(1900) *Life and Letters of Thomas Huxley*, 2 vols, ed. L. Huxley, New York: D. Appleton & Co.

Jokela, J., Dybdahl, M. F., Lively, C. M. (2009) "The maintenance of sex, clonal dynamics and host–parasite coevolution in a mixed population of sexual and asexual snails," *American Naturalist* 174: S43–S53. Online. Available <www.eawag.ch/medien/bulletin/ … /jokela_amnat_2009.pdf>

Kagan, J. (1994) *Galen's Prophecy*, New York: Basic Books.

Kohn, D. (ed.) (1985) *The Darwinian Heritage*, Princeton: Princeton University Press.

Kottler, M. J. (1974) "Alfred Russel Wallace, the origin of man, and spiritualism," *Isis* 65: 145–92.

Lenoir, T. (1989) *The Strategy of Life: Teleology and Mechanics in Nineteenth-Century German Biology*, Chicago: University of Chicago Press.

Lewontin, R., Rose, R., Kamin, L. (1984) *Not in Our Genes*, New York: Pantheon.

Lively, C., Craddock, C., Vrijenboek, R. (1990) "Red queen hypothesis supported by parasitism in sexual and clonal fish," *Nature* 344(6299): 864–66. Online. Available <www.mbari.org/staff/vrijen/PDFS/Lively_EtAl_1990.pdf>

Lyell, C. ([1830–33] 1991) *Principles of geology: Being an inquiry how far the former changes of the earth's surface are referable to causes now in operation*, 3 vols, repr., Chicago: University of Chicago Press.

Lyons, S. (1998) "Science or pseudo-science: Phrenology as a cautionary tale for evolutionary psychology," *Perspectives in Biology and Medicine* 41(4): 491–503.

——(1999) *Thomas Henry Huxley: The Evolution of a Scientist*, Amherst, NY: Prometheus Books.

——(2002) "Thomas Kuhn is alive and well: The evolutionary relationships of simple life forms – A paradigm under siege?" *Perspectives in Biology and Medicine* 45(3): 359–76.

——(2009) *Species, Serpents, Spirits and Skulls: Science at the Margins in the Victorian Age*, New York: SUNY Press.

Malthus, T. (1798) *An Essay on the Principle of Population*, London: J. Johnson.

Marchant, J. (1916) *Alfred Russel Wallace, Letters and Reminiscences*, New York: Harper Brothers.

Margolis, L., Guerrero, R. (1991) "Kingdoms in turmoil," *New Scientist* 129:1761:46–50.

Mayr, E. (1942) *Systematics and the Origin of Species*, New York: Columbia University Press.

——(1982) *The Growth of Biological Thought: Diversity, Evolution and Inheritance*, Cambridge, MA: Belknap Press.

——(1985) "Darwin's five theories of evolution," in D. Kohn (ed.) *The Darwinian Heritage*, Princeton: Princeton University Press.

——(1998) "Two empires or three?" *Proceedings of the National Academy of Science of the United States of America* 95: 9720–23.

Mayr, E., Provine, W. (eds) (1998) *The Evolutionary Synthesis: Perspectives on the Unification of Biology*, Cambridge, MA: Harvard University Press.

McKinney, H. L. (1972) *Wallace and Natural Selection,* New Haven: Yale University Press.

Miller, K. (2007) *Finding Darwin's God: A Scientist's Search for Common Ground between God and Evolution*, New York: Harper Perennial.

Nesse, R. M., Williams, G. C. (1994) *Why We Get Sick: The New Science of Darwinian Medicine*, New York: Times Books.

NICOA (National Indian Council on Aging) (2007) "Stories from *The Pima Indians: Pathfinders for Health*, National Institute of Diabetes and Digestive and Kidney Diseases." Online. Available <www.nicoa.org/Diabetes_Education/aoa_garden/pathfinders/The_Pima_Indian_Pathfinder_for_health.pdf>

Olby, R. ([1974] 1994) *The Path to the Double Helix,* New York: Dover.

Ospovot, D. (1976) "The influence of Karl Ernst von Baer's embryology, 1828–59: A reappraisal in light of Richard Owen and Wiliam B. Carpenter's paleontological application of von Baer's law," *Journal of the History of Biology* 9: 1–28.

——(1981) *The Development of Darwin's Theory: Natural History, Natural Theology, and Natural Selection, 1838–1839,* Cambridge: Cambridge University Press.

Owen, R. (1848) *On the Archetype and Homologies of the Vertebrate Skeleton*, BAAS Report, London: John van Voorst, pp. 178–79.

Pinker, S. (9 February 1998) "Boys will be boys," *New Yorker.*

Plomin, R. (1994) *Genetics and Experience*, Thousand Oaks, CA: Sage.

Proal, A. (February 2008) Interview with evolutionary biologist Paul Ewald. Online. Available <http://bacteriality.com/2008/02/11/ewald/>

Prothero. D. (1992) "Punctuated equilibrium at twenty: A paleontological perspective," *Skeptic* 1(3): 38–47.

Provine, W. (1971) *The Origins of Theoretical Population Genetics*, Chicago: University of Chicago Press.

——(1986) *Sewall Wright: Geneticist and Evolutionist,* Chicago: University of Chicago Press.

Quammen, D. (ed.) (2008) *On the Origin of Species: The Illustrated Edition,* New York: Sterling Press.

Ramachandran, V. S. (2000) "Mirror neurons and imitation learning as the driving force behind 'The great leap forward' in human evolution," *Edge: The Third Culture,* 1 June. Online. Available <www.edge.org>.

——(2007) "The neurology of self-awareness," *Edge: The Third Culture,* 8 January. Online. Available <www.edge.org>

Raup, D. (1992) *Extinction: Bad Genes or Bad Luck?*, New York: W. W. Norton.

Ravi, T. (2010) "Fecal transplant cures chronic gut infection – research in progress." Online. Available <bib.medindia.net/news/fecal-transplant-cures-chronic-gut-infection-microbial-research-in-progress-71343-1.htm#ixzz13aIupZ6F>

Richards, R. (1987) *Darwin and the Emergence of Evolutionary Theories of Mind and Behavior,* Chicago: University of Chicago Press.

Ridley, M. (1993) *The Red Queen,* New York: Macmillan.

Rudwick, M. (1971) "Uniformity and progression: Reflections on the structure of geological theory in the age of Lyell," in D. H. Roller (ed.) *Perspectives in the History of Science and Technology,* Norman: University of Oklahoma Press.

——(1972) *The Meaning of Fossils: Episodes in the History of Paleontology,* New York: Neale Watson Academic; repr. 1982, Chicago: University of Chicago Press.

——(1992) *Scenes from Deep Time,* Chicago: University of Chicago Press.

Rupke, N. (1994) *Richard Owen: Victorian Naturalist,* New Haven: Yale University Press.

Ruse, M., Travis, J. (eds) (2009) *Evolution: The First Four Billion Years,* Cambridge, MA: Belknap Press.

Russell, E. S. ([1916] 1982) *Form and Function: A Contribution to the History of Animal Morphology,* Chicago: University of Chicago Press.

Sapp, J. (2009) *The New Foundations of Evolution: On the Tree of Life,* New York: Oxford University Press.

Simpson, G. G. (1944) *Tempo and Mode in Evolution,* New York: Columbia University Press.

——(1953) *The Major Features of Evolution,* New York: Columbia University Press.

Smith, C. (1999) *Alfred Russel Wallace on Spiritualism, Man and Evolution: An Analytical Essay.* Online. Available <http://people.wku.edu/charles.smith/essays/ARWPAMPH.htm>

Sober, E., Wilson, D. S. (1998) *Unto Others: The Evolution and Psychology of Unselfish Behavior,* Cambridge, MA: Harvard University Press.

Spencer, H. (1904) *An Autobiography,* 2 vols, New York: D. Appleton & Co.

Stanier, R., van Niel, C. B. (1962) "The concept of a bacterium," *Archives of Microbiology* 42: 17–35.

Thompson, D. ([1947] 1961) *On Growth and Form* [abridged], ed. J. Bonner, Cambridge: Cambridge University Press.

Torrey, E. F., Yolken, R. H. (November 2003) "*Toxoplasma gondii* and schizophrenia," *Emerging Infectious Disease.* Serial Online. Available <bib.cdc.gov/ncidod/EID/vol9no11/03–0143.htm>

Wade, N. (2007) *Before the Dawn: Recovering the Lost History of Our Ancestors,* New York: Penguin.

Wallace, A. R. (1864) "The origin of the human races and the antiquity of man deduced from the theory of natural selection," *Journal of the Anthropology Society of London* 2: clviii–clxxxvii. Online. Available <bib.jstor.org/sici?sici= 1356–0131%281864%292%3Cclviii%3ATOOHRA%3E2.0.CO%3B2-D >

——(1869) "Sir Charles Lyell on geological climates and the origin of species," *Quarterly Review* 126: 359–94.

——(1875) "The limits of natural selection as applied to man," *Contributions to the Theory of Natural Selection*, London: Macmillan & Co.

Weiner, J. (1994) *The Beak of the Finch,* New York: Vintage Press.

Wilson, L. (ed.) (1970) *Sir Charles Lyell's Scientific Journals on the Species Question*, New Haven: Yale University Press.

Woese, C. R. (1987) "Bacterial evolution," *Microbiology Review* 51: 221–27.

Woese, C. R., Kandler, O., Wheelis, M. L. (1990) "Towards a natural system of organisms: Proposal for the domains Archaea, Bacteria, and Eucarya," *Proceedings of the National Academy of Sciences of the United States of America* 87: 4576–79. Online. Available <www.pnas.org/content/87/12/4576.full.pdf>

Young, D. (1992) *The Discovery of Evolution,* Cambridge: Cambridge University Press.

Zimmer, C. ([2001] 2006) *Evolution: The Triumph of an Idea*, New York: Harper Perennial.

INDEX